Praise for *Bound Together*

In *Bound Together*, Chris Brauns takes two great theological concepts—union with Christ and union with Adam—and manages to explain them in a way that readers of any level and experience can understand. Highly recommended.

MICHAEL HORTON, author of *The Christian Faith*

No man is an island. But it takes a bold writer to try to convince our hyperindividualistic age. Chris Brauns sketches out a recovery plan informed by God's Word that will help us rebuild the relations so vital to human flourishing and so often forsaken today.

COLLIN HANSEN, editorial director of The Gospel Coalition and author of *Young, Restless, Reformed*

Chris Brauns has done a masterful job of explaining the truth and its implications of the principle of solidarity—what he calls "the principle of the rope." His treatment of all humanity's solidarity with Adam in his sin and the solidarity of all believers with Christ is especially helpful, but the entire book is a masterpiece that will help us understand some of the interpersonal relationships we deal with every day. I highly commend *Bound Together*.

JERRY BRIDGES, author of *The Pursuit of Holiness*

"The rope of the gospel is stronger than the rope of original sin." With these and many other helpful words, author Chris Brauns explores a dimension of life we all crave—communal ties to God, others, and our Savior. I recommend this book to those who see themselves as having these meaningful and enriching ties and those who wish they did. Both will profit from Chris's deep dive into truth—a truth our culture, churches, and selves so desperately need.

STEVE DEWITT, author of *Eyes Wide Open: Enjoying God in Everything*

boundtogether

How We Are Tied to Others
in Good and Bad Choices

chris brauns

ZONDERVAN.com/
AUTHORTRACKER
follow your favorite authors

We want to hear from you. Please send your comments about this book to us in care of zreview@zondervan.com. Thank you.

ZONDERVAN

Bound Together
Copyright © 2013 by Chris Brauns

This title is also available as a Zondervan ebook. Visit www.zondervan.com/ebooks.

Requests for information should be addressed to:

Zondervan, *Grand Rapids, Michigan 49530*

Library of Congress Cataloging-in-Publication Data

Brauns, Chris, 1963-
    Bound together : how we are tied to others in good and bad choices / Chris Brauns.
       p. cm.
     ISBN 978-0-310-49511-6 (pbk.)
     1. Solidarity—Religious aspects—Christianity. I. Title.
    BT738.45.B73 2013
    248.4—dc23   2012034763

All Scripture quotations, unless otherwise indicated, are taken from *The Holy Bible, English Standard Version*, copyright © 2001 by Crossway Bibles, a division of Good News Publishers. Used by permission. All rights reserved.

Scripture quotations marked NIV are taken from The Holy Bible, *New International Version®, NIV®.* Copyright © 1973, 1978, 1984, 2011 by Biblica, Inc.™ Used by permission. All rights reserved worldwide.

Any Internet addresses (websites, blogs, etc.) and telephone numbers in this book are offered as a resource. They are not intended in any way to be or imply an endorsement by Zondervan, nor does Zondervan vouch for the content of these sites and numbers for the life of this book.

Published in association with the literary agency of Credo Communications, LLC, Grand Rapids, MI 49525.

Cover design: *Tammy Johnson*
Cover photography: *Veer / Alloy Photography*
Interior design: *Matthew Van Zomeren*

Printed in the United States of America

---

13 14 15 16 17 18 19 20 /DCI/ 18 17 16 15 14 13 12 11 10 9 8 7 6 5 4 3 2

For Allison, Christopher, Benjamin, and Mary Beth
and all my family —
to whom I am *joyously roped*

Every culture in every age has blind spots and biases that we are often oblivious to, but which are evident to those outside of our culture or time.

Timothy Tennent, *Theology in the Context of World Christianity*

The concept of solidarity ... is basic to the biblical worldview, however alien to our own.

Michael Horton, *The Christian Faith*

Rabbi Simeon bar Yohai taught: There is a story about men who were sitting on a ship, one of them lifted up a borer and began boring a hole beneath his seat. His companions said to him: "What are you sitting and doing?" He replied to them: "What concern is it of yours, am I not drilling under my seat?" They said to him: "But the water will come up and flood the ship for all of us."

Leviticus Rabbah 4.6

The separateness ... which we discern between individuals, is balanced, in absolute reality, by some kind of "inter-inanimation" of which we have no conception at all. It may be that the acts and sufferings of great archetypal individuals such as Adam and Christ are ours, not by legal fiction, metaphor, or causality, but in some much deeper fashion ... There may be a tension between individuality and some other principle.

C. S. Lewis, *The Problem of Pain*

Contents

Foreword by Michael Wittmer 11

Introduction: A Fairy-Tale Beginning 15

PART ONE: UNDERSTANDING THE PRINCIPLE OF THE ROPE

Chapter One: Strange and Troubling Truth 23
The Principle of the Rope in the Bible
If You Still Struggle to Accept the Principle of the Rope

Chapter Two: Original Rope 39
The Doctrine of Original Sin
So What Does All of This Have to Do with Me?
How Was Adam's Sin Transmitted to Us?

Chapter Three: The Rope That Is Stronger 53
The Gospel in Romans 5:12–21

Chapter Four: Bound to a New King 63
Images of Union with Christ

Chapter Five: Can We Blame the Rope? 75
Ezekiel's Response
So Is the Principle of the Rope Real?
Turning from Sin to Follow Christ

PART TWO: APPLYING THE PRINCIPLE OF THE ROPE

Chapter Six: Bound Together for Joy 93

Three Indisputable Truths Regarding Joy
The Problem of Joy
Making the Connection between Joy and
  Corporate Solidarity
Fighting for Joy

Chapter Seven: Bound Together in Marriage 109

Strengthening the Bond of Marriage

Chapter Eight: A Red Rope for Hurting Families 127

Devote All of Jericho to Destruction
The Gospel in the Life of Rahab
Why Did God Order Israel to Kill Everyone in Jericho?
Encouragement for Those Hurting Because of a
  Family Member
All *Christians Have a Family*

Chapter Nine: A Rescue Rope for Those Facing
  the Fear of Death 147

Confidence in the Face of Death from Hebrews 2:10 – 18
The Incarnation
Four Ways Christians Benefit from Their Solidarity with Christ
The Story of Count Helmuth James von Moltke

Chapter Ten: Roped Together in Country and Culture . . . 163

The Rise of American Solidarity
The Problem of Radical Individualism
Why Radical Individualism Persists Today
Why the Church Is Uniquely Qualified to Counter
  Radical Individualism
The Biblical Emphasis on Community
A Final Summary

Afterword 183

Appendix 1: The Gospel and Assurance of Salvation 187
  The Gospel
  The Proper Basis for Assurance of Salvation

Appendix 2: For Further Reading 193
  Original Sin
  Union with Christ
  Biblical and Systematic Theology
  Regarding the Destruction of the Canaanites
  The Church
  On Marriage and the Family
  Sociology and Political History

Acknowledgments 196

Notes 199

Foreword

I first met Chris Brauns the night before our school year began. I was unpacking boxes when he dropped by to see how I was settling in. I had transferred from a larger, well-known seminary, and I was thinking my new school was lucky to have me. Chris was an upperclassman, and he asked if I was taking the Greek placement exam the next day. I replied, with a sniff of disdain, that I didn't think I should need to sit for it, as I had learned Greek at the other place. Chris said my plan would be news to the professor, and he kindly added that I should watch my attitude if I wanted to succeed here.

And just like that, I was introduced to the concept of the rope. Chris cared too much to let me breeze by with an individualistic view of my place in the world. Our seminary didn't exist to serve my career goals. It wasn't merely a stepping-stone to some higher place. It was a community of faculty and students whose lives, for better or worse, would be forever intertwined.

Chris's correction left me in shame — I feared he might think I was arrogant, which, now that I think of it, probably meant I was. But I also realized that Chris's rebuke wasn't pushing me away but pulling me in. He was loosening his strand on the seminary rope to tie me on, and soon enough we would enjoy long talks in the bookstore, listen to each other's practice sermons, and pray for each other's success. The latter was rather lopsided, because I've never met anyone who prays like Chris. He organizes his prayer life like the Puritans arranged their sermons — methodically and as though someone's life depends on it. If Chris tells you he's praying for you, you can be sure that God has heard a compelling case for whatever it is you need.

Still, the rope burns that come from being bound together aren't entirely pleasant. We chafe from the correction of loyal friends, even as we gratefully accept our accountability. We particularly recoil when our solidarity bites from the other direction. Who doesn't resent being roped in with the foolish or sinful actions of our leaders? If the head of your nation declares war on another country, then you're at war too, even if your name is Dietrich Bonhoeffer. And if the head of your race declares war on God, then you're at war too, even if your name is Gandhi.

The apparent unfairness of being lassoed in with the bad choices of others makes the rope decidedly unpopular. And yet, as *Bound Together* winsomely explains, it is our only lifeline. We may dislike the rope, but our hands would be tied without it.

Consider an alternate world in which the rope does not exist: No one is harmed by Adam's sin and everyone begins life with a fresh start. What are the odds that you and I would keep our slates clean? Would you want the pressure of choosing God every moment of your life, knowing that one proud or lustful thought would damn you forever (Matthew 5:27 – 30)? And without the rope, what could pull us out of the pit we would invariably dig for ourselves?

Back in the real world, our inheritance of Adam's sin guarantees we will fail. But the same rope that binds us to Adam's guilt and corruption also enables us to be tied to the last Adam, Jesus Christ. So the rope doesn't merely strangle us with someone else's sin; it's also our only shot at salvation.

Ultimately *Bound Together* is a grammar book for the gospel.

It explains how the gospel works and why our individualistic age lacks the basic syntax to make sense of it. The presumed rightness of individualism implies that the individual is right, for no one wants more of a bad thing. Our culture's belief in our individual goodness prompts therapists to counsel bored wives to "follow their heart," even when it leads away from their marriage, and reality television stars to defiantly announce they're going to unleash their loud and obnoxious selves — and if others don't like it, well, that's on them.

The gospel shushes such narcissistic applause, for the cross would not have been necessary if we were already good people. Jesus did not die to make nice people a little nicer or so repressed people could learn to more fully appreciate themselves. Jesus died for us, condemned sinners who are doomed without the miraculous intervention of God. And the God who saved us from ourselves has not left us to ourselves. He weaves our souls together, looping our lives around Jesus and knotting them in the gospel.

You may never come to love the rope. There are still aspects of it that rub me the wrong way. But you won't read too far into *Bound Together* before you'll realize how much you need it. With any luck, you'll begin to think about the rope as Winston Churchill felt about democracy: "Democracy is the worst form of government, except for all the others." The rope is better than democracy, and a thousand times more redemptive. It's how God has chosen to govern his world, and how he has chosen to save you.

If we want to understand the gospel, we'll have to think more like a Christian and less like an American. *Bound Together* will open our eyes to the difference.

Michael Wittmer,
Grand Rapids Theological Seminary

A Fairy-Tale Beginning

This is exactly the message that fairy tales get across to the child in manifold form: that a struggle against severe difficulties in life is unavoidable, is an intrinsic part of human existence—but that if one does not shy away, but steadfastly meets unexpected and often unjust hardships, one masters all obstacles and at the end emerges victorious.

Modern stories written for young children mainly avoid these existential problems, although they are crucial issues for all of us ... The fairy tale ... confronts the child squarely with the basic human predicaments.

Bruno Bettelheim, *The Uses of Enchantment*

Laying out the evidence that we are bound together is easy. Convincing you to follow this trail of clues where it leads is the hard part. Nevertheless, persuading you to carefully investigate the reality that we are deeply connected to one another is my goal in writing this book. I want to assure you that, if you do, you will discover truth that is fundamental to all true joy, however dark it may seem in the beginning. Indeed, without the truth that we are bound together there is no joy. So follow the clues where they lead. You won't be disappointed.

I will say much more about how we are bound together in chapter 1. For now, you need only consider situations in which the decisions of one person affect the future of other persons, as though they are figuratively roped together.

Sadly, negative examples usually come to mind first.

Perhaps you have rebellious children, and the consequences and concerns that they have brought to your family hang like a lodestone about your neck.

Maybe you are married to an abusive or unfaithful spouse, and for you, life is an open wound.

If you are the child of abuse, you have scar tissue on your heart, not through your own fault, but because one or both of your parents made despicable decisions, however long ago it may have been.

Or we might approach this trail of clues from the opposite direction. Maybe you were the one who made poor decisions that had disastrous consequences for someone else. You struggle with the guilt of realizing that you caused suffering for your children or parents.

Perhaps the examples that make you shake your head are not so personal. Have you ever wondered why God allows bombs to explode on children when they have nothing to do with the politics involved?

As I have already acknowledged, these are negative examples. It hurts to consider that people suffer because of decisions made by someone else. Indeed, it is so painful to contemplate that, more often than not, people choose the ostrich's approach of burying their heads in the sand rather than looking this reality square in the eye. We would rather not meditate on an aspect of life that seems so unfair. How can it be that a three-year-old little girl suffers because of decisions her parents made?

But here's the thing. As negative as it may seem in the beginning, the truth that we are bound together with others offers a trail of clues about how life works. *If you follow this trail where it leads, you can be assured that you will discover a truth that is foundational to life and to the greatest news ever shared.*

Think of investigating the idea that we are bound together like a fairy tale. Fairy tales end well. Famously so. You know the clichés: "fairy-tale ending" and "happily ever after." Jack chops down the beanstalk. A prince awakens Snow White with a kiss. Dorothy realizes that the end of the rainbow was in Kansas all along.

But if a "fairy-tale ending" is clichéd because "they all live happily ever after," fairy-tale beginnings are an altogether different matter. Fairy tales open deep in the woods. No sooner has the storyteller said "once upon a time" than the cyclone heads for Kansas and the wicked stepsisters begin tormenting Cinderella. Indeed, the principal aim of the first couple of pages of a fairy tale is to instill something just short of terror in the child who is listening. Picture the horrific difficulties your average fairy-tale protagonist faces. Little Red Riding Hood's invalid grandmother lives on the other side of a wolf-infested forest. A troll lurks under the bridge that the three Billy Goats Gruff must cross if they are to avoid slowly starving. Lacking GPS, Hansel and Gretel implement a flawed method for finding their way home, and it is their bad fortune to do so a stone's throw from the cottage of a witch who eats children — but only after boiling them first.

Predictably, some suggest we should opt for a bland version of the story where the Big Bad Wolf only chases the first two little pigs. I don't know about you, but I'm not buying what they're selling. What a colorless land our children would visit if, for fear of thorns in the beginning, we never shared the thrill of good news at the end.

Insurmountable odds and grave danger make fairy tales work.

My little daughter Mary Beth pleads with me to read fairy tales to her, no matter how scared she may get. Sometimes she even hides under the blanket. But she has never asked me to quit before "happily ever after." She stays because she is rightly convinced that, however wicked the stepmother may be, the story will end well. There is the promise that things will get better and that, as Frederick Buechner writes, "happiness is both inevitable and endless" in fairy tales.[1] Though she cannot put it into words, Mary Beth intuitively understands that the light at the end of a fairy tale will shine all the brighter for having started so deep in the forest.

This book is like a fairy tale both in how it ends and how it begins, only to a greater degree. A worse beginning. A better ending. The beginning is brutal, worse than a fairy tale because it's real, and more troubling, because as children of the modern individualistic age, we resent that it is so. But I assure you that it concludes well — gloriously so, infinitely better than any fairy tale. It has a last page that only God, who can do immeasurably more than all we can ask or imagine, could make up.

In fact, you don't have to wait until the last page for the good news to begin. By chapter 3, the Prince will make his entrance.

You've been warned. The first two chapters are grim. Don't give up. Hide under the blankets if you must. But make the trek through the woods. It's necessary if you want to fully grasp the glory of the good news that follows. However strange and offensive the principles and truths we will unpack may seem at first, I promise you that they can become your lifeline for joy in this life and the basis for "happily ever after" in the next.

To "once upon a time" we now turn.

PART 1

UNDERSTANDING THE PRINCIPLE OF THE ROPE

CHAPTER ONE

Strange and Troubling Truth

The funny thing about the truly strange is that sometimes it's real.

Alan Jacobs, *Wayfaring*

Everyone will have noticed how the Old Testament seems at times to ignore our conception of the individual.

C. S. Lewis, *The Problem of Pain*

And Joshua and all Israel with him took Achan the son of Zerah, and the silver and the cloak and the bar of gold, *and his sons and daughters and his oxen and donkeys and sheep and his tent and all that he had*. And they brought them up to the Valley of Achor. And Joshua said, "Why did you bring trouble on us? The LORD brings trouble on you today." And all Israel stoned him with stones. They burned them with fire and stoned them with stones.

Joshua 7:24–25, emphasis added

I didn't understand the principle of the rope was at work when I saw Stevie Baxter drunk. As far as that goes, at first I didn't even know he was drunk. I was only ten at the time. Stevie was eleven. I was playing with friends in a green meadow by the muddy Des Moines River. Stevie was sipping what appeared to be orange pop and acting stupid. I figured he was staggering around and slurring his words to entertain us.*

My friends, Stevie's cousins, were far more knowledgeable about the effects of alcohol than I was, and they immediately understood that Stevie was three sheets to the wind. They laughed and poked one another. I sensed I was missing something, but I couldn't quite figure it out.

Even when I saw Stevie getting sick, I didn't know what was going on. It wasn't until Stevie's mother showed up and figured out that Stevie's older brothers had spiked her eleven-year-old's Orange Crush that I put two and two together.

Mrs. Baxter lit into Stevie's suppliers with the unmitigated fury of a tornado. I was scared just *watching* her scream and yell. The objects of Mrs. Baxter's wrath hung their heads and took the verbal pummeling. They were too drunk themselves to be much offended. All the while, Stevie was bent over, hands on his knees, continuing to vomit on the banks of the muddy river.

---

*I've changed some of the details of this story so it does not precisely correspond to one situation.

I didn't tell my parents that Stevie had been drunk. But if I had shared it with them, despite the fact that he was eleven years old at the time, they would have been only mildly surprised. Stevie was a Baxter. Baxters drank. It was expected. Your average Baxter child was regularly in trouble by the end of junior high and had crashed at least one car by the time he was in his late teens. Of course, not *every* Baxter was drunk *all* the time. But most were. Stevie was just the latest in a long line of drunken dominoes to topple over.

Like I said, I didn't understand at the time that the principle of the rope was at work. If you had asked me at ten years old what had happened, I would have said that Stevie chose to be "bad," that it was his decision to drink. And if you had asked me why I wasn't drunk, I would have told you it was because I had made better decisions than Stevie, that somehow my ability to say no to alcohol was stronger than Stevie's, that I was a better person in some way.

Even without knowing any of the people involved in this story, you can tell this is an overly simplistic evaluation. The reality — a truth we will be unpacking in greater detail in this book — is that Stevie's decision to drink at age eleven was not merely the result of his choices as an individual. Yes, at some point Stevie chose to drink. But a large part of the reason Stevie guzzled whatever was mixed with his orange pop was that the people in his family had shown him by their words and examples that this was the only choice he *could* make. Stevie's family had jumped into the river of alcoholism. And when they did, they pulled Stevie into the current after them.

Families like Stevie's are but one sad example among billions. And the reality that underlies this experience — that our lives, our decisions, our choices, our actions are directly and indirectly affected by the decisions and choices of other people — is one of the defining realities of life. Yet much of the time, we forget about it. We act as if we are the captains of our own ships, as if somehow our lives and decisions as individuals can remain unaffected by our ethnicity, our family background, and our nationality.

In the case of families, we might even say that "they are we and we are they." Our future and our place in this world aren't *simply* the sum of our own individual choices. On varying levels, we are roped together with others. When someone we are roped to is lifted up, we are lifted up with them. When he or she jumps off a figurative cliff, we are pulled down with them. This is what I refer to as the "principle of the rope" — the simple truth that our lives, choices, and actions are linked to the lives, choices, and actions of other people. To put it simply, as I have done in the title of this book, we are "bound together," tied to others in our good and bad choices.

There are endless illustrations of this principle, and not all are so dramatic. We talk a lot about the principle of the rope in our church and at home. Recently, when I was out for a walk with my ten-year-old son, I asked him, "Benjamin, what do I mean by the principle of the rope?" He responded quickly. "Oh, I think about that a lot. Here's the best example I can give. Today a couple of kids in my class got in trouble. So none of us got to go out for recess. That's the principle of the rope."

So it is. While my son's fourth-grade class is comprised of individuals, they are not islands unto themselves. When Ben's classmates misbehaved, they were "roped" to the rest of the class. Two jumped off the behavioral cliff. And, at least for one recess, they pulled the rest of the class down with them. As this classroom example implies, the principle of the rope — our solidarity with one another as human beings — is not confined to our family relationships. It applies to institutions like the church and the government as well. When Hitler chose to be an evil dictator, he pulled the entire nation of Germany over the cliff with him. Of course, specific *individuals* were complicit in this evil. But can we blame young children who happened to belong to German families during this time in history for the sins committed by their parents? Surely it was just their misfortune to be "roped" to the Third Reich. And yet the fact remains that these children, however innocent they may have been, still faced the consequences of decisions made by those who came before them. Though not directly responsible for the crimes committed, their lives were linked to their national identity, and the choices and decisions made by their parents and leaders changed their future.

I use the phrase "the principle of the rope" to help people picture this reality of how connected we are to one another. Theologians refer to this principle in several different ways. Sometimes they speak of "corporate identity" or of "the one and the many," referring to how the actions of one individual can affect many others. Just as often, the principle of the rope is referenced by the word *solidarity* — one of those words we often hear used without considering what it means. *Solidarity* refers to a union of interests, purposes, or sympathies among members of a group. It speaks to the ties that bind a group together. You may have heard the word *solidarity* used in the context of labor unions. When union leaders appeal to their members to show solidarity during a labor dispute, they are calling for members to show that they are bound together as a unified whole.

In this book, I will be using phrases like "the principle of the rope" and "corporate solidarity" and the word *solidarity* interchangeably. As a pastor, I try hard to make abstract theological concepts concrete and accessible to people, so I often prefer the simpler phrase "the principle of the rope." But at times, I will use the more technical language for precision. In every case, these phrases refer to the same reality.

I am not the first person to use the image of rope as a picture of the invisible connections that exist between human beings. In the great American novel titled *Moby Dick*, Herman Melville's Ishmael reflected on these realities as well. Two men named Ishmael and Queequeg are cutting up a whale they have just killed. Ishmael remains on the boat, but he is "roped" to Queequeg, who is down in the water on the back of the mostly submerged whale. Should Queequeg begin to be drawn under the whale, it is Ishmael's job to jerk his comrade upright. But this is a precarious connection. If for some reason Queequeg is pulled under the whale, Ishmael will inevitably be pulled along with him, and they will both drown. Reflecting on his state of being roped to another man, Ishmael comes to see that the literal rope connecting them pictures a far older, much stronger rope that connects all people together:

> I say, I saw that this situation of mine was the precise situation of every mortal that breathes; only, in most cases he, one way or other, has this … [roped] connexion with a plurality of other mortals. If your banker breaks, you snap; if your apothecary by mistake sends you poison in your pills, you die.[1]

Melville's Ishmael didn't like the principle of the rope. He felt there was injustice in the principle, that it was wrong for some to suffer because of the poor decisions of others.[2] And yet he could not escape the clear truth that he saw: for better or for worse, we are roped together.

Like Ishmael, I struggled with the fairness of the principle of the rope. How could it be right that when a grown man chooses to be violent, a three-year-old little girl suffers? For me, this idea didn't sit very well. But this was before I realized that this principle, which seems so terrible on the one hand, is our lifeline to joy. I'll get to why the principle of the rope is such glorious news. At this point, my goal isn't to convince you about whether or not the principle of the rope is fair or whether it's good news. Instead, the first objective is to establish agreement that solidarity is an undeniable aspect of reality.

We could draw a parallel between the principle of the rope and the law of gravity. With regard to gravity, it doesn't seem fair to me, and I don't understand it. Gravity has been hard on me since I was a youth. Growing up, it was my life's dream to become a star basketball player. I lived on a farm, and like a scene out of the movie *Hoosiers*, my parents set up a hoop for me to practice on. Even though our driveway was gravel and it was hard to dribble the ball, I would shoot baskets for long hours each day. Eventually, I could knock down shots from all over the driveway.

Yet, despite my hours of practice, the law of gravity brought an early end to my basketball-playing career. I was around four foot ten at that time, and though I would try as hard as I could to jump, I could never quite leap high enough off the hardwood to slam the ball through the hoop. As a matter of fact, my vertical jump was so pathetic that I had a hard time even touching the net. In the sixth grade I signed with the Parsons Chevrolet franchise in Keosauqua, Iowa, and we struggled through a mediocre season. Padget's Gadgets crushed us in both the regular season and the play-offs. To this day, I blame our dismal season on the law of gravity.

Eventually, I went to college and took physics, where we spent a great deal of time *studying* gravity. We learned about a brilliant British guy named Henry Cavendish, who was the first to accurately measure the gravitational constant. Our class experimented with dropping objects off tall buildings. I memorized formulas and figured out the mass of the moon and earth based on the gravitational pull. To this day I don't understand how gravity works. And as I have gotten slower and even more vertically challenged in my old age, I continue to resent it.

You know where I am going. Regardless of whether or not I agree with the fairness of the law of gravity, or understand it, I still live in light of it. I'm not planning on walking off the fourth floor of a building anytime soon, and it isn't up to me to decide what is fair. This is our Father's world. The principle of the rope is part of it. I rest in his justice.

Of course, if we are really going to consider the validity of the point, we need to look at the Bible. What does God's Word say about the principle of the rope? Are people treated as individual units? Or are they roped to one another?

The Principle of the Rope in the Bible

Time and again, as we read through Scripture, we find examples that validate the reality of the principle of the rope. In fact, when I first began to study the Bible, one of the most difficult things to accept was how often innocent people, particularly young children, suffered because of the decisions made by someone else.

For example, consider the story of the flood in Genesis 7:9 – 19. We read that God destroyed all people on the earth through a flood, with one notable exception — the family of Noah. Apart from Noah's immediate family, every single person on earth died in a disaster that made Hurricane Katrina look like a spring shower. Genesis 7:22 tells us that "everything on the dry land in whose nostrils was the breath of life died," and this includes all the small children who were not part of Noah's family. Please understand, I know the Bible tells us these people were wicked and corrupt. But how much chance did the three-year-olds of that day have to turn things around before they drowned? Why didn't God have the toddlers walk up the ramp of the ark, two by two? The only answer that makes sense is that young children drowned in the flood *because they were roped together with their parents and their culture.* In other words, when God punished people in the flood, he wasn't just dealing with them as individuals; he was treating them as people corporately accountable to him.

In a similar manner, we see that the children of Sodom and Gomorrah were roped together with their cities in judgment. In Genesis 19:23 – 29, we read that God wiped Sodom and Gomorrah off the face of the map. After God's judgment, when Abraham looked toward the land of the valley, he saw that "the smoke of the land went up like the smoke of a furnace" (Genesis 19:28). Everyone in those cities, with the exception of Lot's family, burned — children included.

Later, in the book of Exodus, we read that God punished the entire nation of Egypt because of decisions made by their representative leader, Pharaoh (Exodus 7 – 14). When the Nile turned to blood, three-year-olds were thirsty. Swarms of gnats descended on four-year-olds. It was not only Pharaoh and his minions who got boils, but *all* the Egyptians (Exodus 9:11). Firstborn sons died, regardless of their age during the Passover, from the firstborn of the pharaoh who sat on the throne to the firstborn of the prisoner in the dungeon (Exodus 12:29). There was loud wailing in the land because there was not one household where there was not someone dead. When Egypt pursued the children of Israel into the desert, soldiers drowned in the Red Sea while following orders (Exodus 14:28).

Or consider God's command to the Israelites to completely wipe out the people of the land of Canaan. Of Israel's first battle with Jericho, we read, "Then they devoted all in the city to destruction, both men and women, young and old, oxen, sheep, and donkeys, with the edge of the sword" (Joshua 6:21). If you are like me, you may read this and object: "Surely there must have been varying degrees of wickedness in Jericho, at least by human standards. Why was everyone destroyed?" Yet the Bible is clear on this matter. With the exception of Rahab and her family, everyone and everything in Jericho was destroyed. Have you honestly considered what it looked like and felt like for the Israelite soldiers to execute entire families? How could God hold the children accountable for the sins of their parents?

Lest we accuse God of favoring his own people over others, we should note that we find evidence of God's own people suffering for the sins and choices of others in the story that follows the battle of Jericho. When Achan, an Israelite, violated the covenant and stole some of the devoted things following the battle of Jericho, God allowed the entire nation of Israel to lose the next battle they fought against the city of Ai. In Joshua 7:1, we read, "The people of Israel broke faith in regard to the devoted things, for Achan the son of Carmi, son of Zabdi, son of Zerah, of the tribe of Judah, took some of the devoted things. And the anger of the LORD burned against the people of Israel."

To be clear: as the result of what *one man*, Achan, did, *many* Israelites died when they took up arms to fight, as God had commanded them, in the next battle of the military campaign to take the Promised Land (Joshua 7:2 – 5). It was not until Joshua inquired of the Lord as to why they had lost the battle that the Lord informed him of the problem. Because Achan had taken the things devoted to destruction, God punished Israel as a whole (Joshua 7:10 – 11). In other words, thirty-six soldiers died in that battle, not because of their own sin, but because they were roped together with Achan. The reality of their corporate solidarity as a nation — the principle of the rope — meant that the sin of one man had a direct effect on the rest of the nation. Mothers had to explain to children that they would never know their father, all because someone *else* had sinned.

We see additional examples throughout the Old Testament, and in many cases they also reflect a cultural concept of solidarity. In the ancient world, the idea that families were bound together seems to have been assumed. We see it in the book of Daniel when, after Daniel is rescued from the mouths of lions, the men who maliciously accused Daniel are fed to the lions instead (Daniel 6:24). But there is a detail you might be inclined to read past or ignore when you share this story with your children. Not only were the evil men punished, but their *wives and children* were fed to the lions as well. God spared Daniel, because Daniel "trusted in his God" (Daniel 6:23). But no angel showed up to close the jaws of the lions before they devoured the children of the guilty. The text reads, "The king commanded, and those men who had maliciously accused Daniel were brought and cast into the den of lions — they, their children, and their wives. And before they reached the bottom of the den, the lions overpowered them and broke all their bones in pieces" (Daniel 6:24).

A friend of mine told me recently that a third grader in a Sunday school class at her church had pointed this out. The teacher, at a loss as to how to respond, simply let the class know they weren't going to discuss that today. While I don't blame the teacher for avoiding that difficult conversation, at some point we should stop and ask, "Why *do* such things happen?"

Throughout the Scriptures, we also see that the principle of the rope is repeatedly observed when *the decisions and choices made by God's representative leaders have consequences for their people.* Consider 2 Samuel 24:1 – 17. Seventy thousand Israelite men died because King David sinfully decided to count his troops. It is hard to comprehend exactly why David's census was so evil, though it may have been evidence of pride or arrogance in David's heart. Yet regardless of why it was wrong, we can tell, based on the severe judgment inflicted by God, that it was truly awful in God's sight. God's anger against Israel was kindled, and seventy thousand Israelite men died (2 Samuel 24:15). And all of this happened, not because these people had sinned in any particular way, but because David, their king, had sinned. David understood this, and he even pointed it out as he pleaded with God for mercy (2 Samuel 24:17).

Time after time in the Scriptures we see a common principle at work: *the choices, words, and actions of one person represent many others.* Solidarity has always existed among groups of people, from the beginning of the world. We see this in God's judgment against sin and in his decision to destroy the world by flood. We see it in his punishment of the Israelites, the Egyptians, and the people of

Jericho. Apart from the idea of solidarity, how can we explain what we see, either in Scripture or in the common experiences of life?

No doubt, you can easily list any number of examples. You probably know someone whose children have made terrible decisions, and now, in some measure, the entire family has been affected. You may know of someone who married, and over time the decisions of their spouse have done great damage to them and those they love. As much as we may like to believe we are individuals responsible solely for our own decisions, our experience tells a different story. We observe the principle of the rope in life, and it is evident in the Bible.

If You Still Struggle to Accept the Principle of the Rope

Not everyone is willing to accept something as true just because they find it in the Bible. I recall reading a post written by a young mother whose eleven-year-old daughter was very upset that all of Achan's family was stoned when he sinned at Jericho:

> We've been reading through Joshua in school (we homeschool). Last week, when my eleven-year-old daughter read about Achan's sin and his punishment in chapter 7, she burst into tears. The thought of God killing Achan's wife and children as a result of HIS sin did not sit well with her. We talked about God's reasons for it, but they were insufficient for her. It didn't seem fair, and I had to agree with her. She confessed that serving, believing in, following a God like that didn't appeal to her. Our discussion and my husband and my answers didn't seem to clarify or comfort her.
>
> Honestly, we were both at a loss for a clear answer ...
>
> How do you respond to an eleven-year-old who doesn't care about wrath, holiness, etc., and sees God as a big bully and unjust? I would really appreciate any responses and insight.[3]

The last time I checked, there were sixty-eight comments weighing in on how this mother should respond to her daughter. The options recommended included:

- *Deny the authority of the Bible.* Several comments suggested that the events didn't really happen the way they are recorded in the Bible.
- *Ignore the Old Testament and focus on the New Testament.* One father commented, "I don't tend to spend a great deal of time with my children on the Old Testament."

For those who believe in the authority of Scripture and the ongoing importance of understanding both the Old and New Testament writings as the inspired Word of God, neither of these options is good. If we hold that the Bible is God's Word then we believe it has something to teach us, that it contains truth we need to understand. The most self-defeating thing we can do is to deny the grace God has extended to us through his precious, authoritative Word.[4]

Let me give you a different alternative. Rather than being driven away from God by our discomfort with something we encounter in life and his Word, we should run to him. God is not only just; he is also loving, merciful, and gracious. We need not fear those portions of his Word that seem difficult to understand.

Indeed, it may even be that our discomfort indicates a place where our understanding needs to be corrected the most. This may well be the case with the idea of solidarity. It is a basic aspect of the biblical worldview largely misunderstood by the modern Western mind. This is a point that Michael Horton makes. He writes, "The concept of solidarity ... is basic to the biblical worldview, however alien to our own."[5] We hesitate to consider solidarity because it seems so strange. Yet, if it is basic to the biblical worldview, we must study it, and do so thoroughly.

My challenge is that you will make it a goal to understand

biblically what the principle of the rope is all about. If you do that, you will see it is fundamental to all hope and joy.

But not quite yet. Before we get to the good news that brings us hope and joy, we need to reflect further on the negative side of being bound together with others. What is the ultimate negative example of the principle of the rope?

CHAPTER TWO

Original
Rope

In ADAM'S Fall
We sinned all.

The New England Primer

Solidarity of the human race under Adamic headship is the source both of the grandeur and of the tragedy of our existence.

Michael Horton, *The Christian Faith*

Therefore, as one trespass led to condemnation for all men ...

Romans 5:18

Apart from the principle of the rope, it is impossible to understand the course of human history. I understand that a statement like this invites debate. If you're like me, when an author introduces to you some hidden key that unlocks the meaning of life, you immediately raise your eyebrows and mentally push back. Nevertheless, I am prepared to stand by my claim.

To review, the principle of the rope is simply the truth that we human beings are not *strictly* autonomous individuals. Rather, we are bound to one another in corporate relationships. To various degrees, we are *represented* by the choices, actions, and decisions of others, and they, likewise, are affected or represented by ours. We are united to others, in our good and in our bad decisions. As we saw in the last chapter, there are examples of this kind of solidarity throughout the Bible and history.

The idea that we are deeply connected to other people, even people we may have never met and do not know, sounds a bit strange and offensive to our modern ears. How, for instance, can it be fair for three-year-old children to be drowned in a flood because of sinful decisions made by their families? Yet, as strange and offensive as the principle of the rope may sound to our culturally conditioned sensibilities, without a firm grasp of this truth it is impossible to understand the course of human history and the story line of the Bible.

The Doctrine of Original Sin

We first encounter the reality of solidarity "in the beginning."
"In the beginning," Genesis 1 tells us, in six successive days, by
divine fiat, God spoke all of creation into existence. The first
thing to notice about God's creation in Genesis 1 is that it was
"good." The Hebrew word translated "good" means "excellent of
its kind."[1] Genesis 1 repeatedly stresses that by God's own assessment, creation was exactly as it should be (Genesis 1:4, 10, 12,
18, 21, 25).

Scripture tells us that the sixth day of the creation was even
better than the first five. After each of the first five days of creation, God says that creation is "good"; only at the end of the sixth
day, with the introduction of humanity, does God pronounce it
"very good." Given the beauty of our Father's world, we may wonder why God reserved the words "very good" for the introduction
of Adam and Eve. Thankfully, Scripture tells us why.

> Then God said, "Let us make man in our image, after our
> likeness. And let them have dominion over the fish of the sea
> and over the birds of the heavens and over the livestock and
> over all the earth and over every creeping thing that creeps
> on the earth."
>
> Genesis 1:26

Humanity was the high point of God's created order because
only humans are created in the image of God. This is the repeated
stress in three parallel lines of Hebrew poetry in Genesis 1:27.

> So God created man in his own image,
>   in the image of God he created him;
>   male and female he created them.

Two words are used as synonyms in this context ("image"
and "likeness"). The first means "to carve" or "to cut."[2] The second usually refers to external appearance.[3] Theologian Herman
Bavinck explains the significance of our creation in God's image:

Man does not simply bear or have the image of God; he is the image of God.

From the doctrine that man has been created in the image of God flows the clear implication that image extends to man in his entirety. Nothing in man is excluded from the image of God. All creatures reveal traces of God, but only man is the image of God. And he is that image totally, in soul and body, in all faculties and powers, in all conditions and relationships. Man is the image of God because and insofar as he is true man, and he is man, true and real man, because and insofar as he is the image of God.[4]

God's plan for his image bearers was not that they simply lounge around the garden of Eden in hammocks sipping tropical drinks. Instead, they were given a special mandate. It is a beautiful text to read.

And God blessed them. And God said to them, "Be fruitful and multiply and fill the earth and subdue it, and have dominion over the fish of the sea and over the birds of the heavens and over every living thing that moves on the earth." And God said, "Behold, I have given you every plant yielding seed that is on the face of all the earth, and every tree with seed in its fruit. You shall have them for food. And to every beast of the earth and to every bird of the heavens and to everything that creeps on the earth, everything that has the breath of life, I have given every green plant for food." And it was so. And God saw everything that he had made, and behold, it was very good. And there was evening and there was morning, the sixth day.

Genesis 1:28 – 31

Theologians call the charge that Adam and Eve were given "the creation mandate" or "the cultural mandate." Based on the prototype of the garden of Eden, God's image bearers were to rule over and subdue all the earth extending the garden of Eden. In so doing, they would glorify God and enjoy perfect fellowship with him.

The words used in this passage, "subdue" and "have dominion over," are associated with a royal or kingly task. Adam and Eve were to reign over creation as God's special vice-regents, his appointed royalty. They were created in God's image as his special representatives. In performing their royal commission, Adam and Eve were free to enjoy creation — with one restriction. They were not to eat from the tree of the knowledge of good and evil. It was a tremendously liberating restriction: "You may surely eat of *every* tree of the garden, but of the tree of the knowledge of good and evil you shall not eat, for in the day that you eat of it you shall surely die" (Genesis 2:16 – 17, emphasis added). Adam and Eve could enjoy all of creation, virtually everything God had made, except for the one tree that was forbidden. God had given them the opportunity to volitionally demonstrate their commitment to him.

Adam and Eve's mandate was not without obstacles. Satan, the great deceiver and enemy of God's purposes, was on the prowl. If Adam and Eve were to be successful in fulfilling their call, then it was necessary for them to resist his wiles. Instead of listening to the word of Satan, "[Adam] was to rule over and subdue the serpent, which was to be reflective of God's own activity in Gen. 1 of subduing the chaotic darkness of creation and ruling over it by his word."[5]

Yet we know this is not what happened. Tragically, despite God's great blessing, Adam and Eve chose to sin. Rather than trusting in God's word, they listened to the half-truths and twisted lies of the serpent and ate from the tree of the knowledge of good and evil. The consequences of their actions were swift and severe. As the table below summarizes, Adam and Eve's sin tainted and twisted every aspect of their identity. It corrupted and frustrated the tasks they had been given by God. Worship of God gave way to idolatry. Love of neighbor gave way to hatred. Caring for creation was replaced by pollution and decay.

Aspect of "Image of God"	Legitimate Expression	Examples of How Sin Twisted
Worship: Relating to God	A love and desire for God that organize every aspect of life	Genesis 3:22–23: idolatry —substituting other gods, pride, selfishness
Community: Relating to Humanity	The marriage relationship and children	Genesis 3:16: all forms of sexual sin, pain in bearing children, divorce and troubled marriages
	Relating within community	Interpersonal conflict, racism, gangs, gossip, cliques, wars
Vice-Regency: Relating to Creation	Humanity is to represent God and exercise care and responsibility over creation.	Genesis 3:17–18: thorns and thistles, toilsome nature of work, pollution

Table 1: How Original Sin Affected All of Creation and Human History

Michael Horton summarizes how Adam's sin twisted every good work he had been given to do:

> Adam's role as false witness bears relation not only to God but to the whole creation, since he represents all human beings and humankind collectively as the chief of the rulers over the other creaturely realms. The creation had been placed at the disposal of Adam in a state of integrity, with a commission to be a steward. But now this power, too, is twisted by a perversity of will. Royal stewardship is twisted into tyranny. Every sign of human oppression, violence, idolatry, and immorality in the world can be seen as the perversion of an original good. The commission to be fruitful and to multiply, to work in, guard, protect, and subdue God's garden so that its peace and righteousness extend to the ends of the earth is twisted into empires of oppression in order to secure a consummation without God.[6]

So What Does All of This Have to Do with Me?

Now if you're like me, the account of Adam and Eve in Genesis 1 – 3 seems very remote. Ancient history. Looking at the world today, I have trouble imagining the untainted beauty of the garden of Eden — a perfect Paradise of trees and water and animals.

Yet as far away and remote as the events of Eden may seem to us living east of Eden today, Adam and Eve's sin was anything but irrelevant. Their mandate was more than just a private command for two individuals. As is always the case with royalty, the choices that Adam and Eve made had consequences, not only for themselves, but for their entire kingdom — their descendants and the land they had been given to rule. Everything God had given to them was affected by their actions.

The consequences of Adam and Eve's sin, which we continue to live with today, are summarized in a doctrine — a teaching of the church commonly referred to as "original sin." Original sin refers to the reality that we are all bound to Adam in his choice to disobey God's command. Because we are bound to Adam by the principle of the rope, when Adam sinned against God, he pulled himself and his descendants into a chasm of sickness, perversion, corruption, and decay that continue to rule our world today. Alan Jacobs has described the consequences of Adam's sin like cracks spreading across a pane of glass, deepening until they eventually shattered all of humanity.[7]

The label "original sin" sometimes confuses people. Many people erroneously believe it refers only to Adam and Eve's decision to eat from the tree of the knowledge of good and evil in the garden of Eden. But the doctrine isn't just a reference to the first sin. Rather, original sin refers to the *result* of Adam and Eve's sin as well. The Westminster Confession of Faith summarizes this well:

> By this sin they fell from their original righteousness and communion, with God, and so became dead in sin, and wholly defiled in all the parts and faculties of soul and body.

> They being the root of all mankind, *the guilt of this sin was imputed; and the same death in sin, and corrupted nature, conveyed to all their posterity descending from them by ordinary generation.*
>
> From this original corruption, whereby we are utterly indisposed, disabled, and made opposite to all good, and wholly inclined to all evil, do proceed all actual transgressions.
>
> This corruption of nature, during this life, does remain in those that are regenerated; and although it be, through Christ, pardoned, and mortified; yet both itself, and all the motions thereof, are truly and properly sin.[8]

Broadly speaking, there are two consequences to Adam's rebellion. First, Adam and all his descendants are *guilty* of sinning against God, and second, all of Adam's descendants inherit a *corrupted nature*. This means that all human beings, including babies and small children, are not innocent victims of circumstance. They are born sinners. As David confessed in Psalm 51:5, "Behold, I was brought forth in iniquity, and in sin did my mother conceive me." The problem we face as Adam's descendants is not that we are sinners because we sin; rather, we sin because we are sinners.

How Was Adam's Sin Transmitted to Us?

But how is it that Adam's sin is inherited? If it is true that we are "roped" to Adam, what is the nature of the rope that ties us to him? Let me warn you that we are heading into some deeper waters here. John Calvin, in his commentary on Psalm 51, declined to enter into the mysterious discussion of how Adam's sin was transmitted, simply writing that "it is enough that we hold, that Adam, upon his fall was despoiled of his original righteousness, his reason darkened, his will perverted, and that, being reduced to this state of corruption, he brought children into the world resembling himself in character."[9]

Calvin was correct to warn us against trying to comprehend everything about the transmission of Adam's sin. In trying to understand the doctrine of original sin, we must not go further than what Scripture teaches.[10] So while it is worthwhile and necessary to ponder the nature of how Adam's sin was transmitted, we need to be cautious in the conclusions we draw.

Among Bible-believing Christians throughout history, two general views have prevailed to explain exactly how Adam's sin was transmitted. The two views are referred to as the *realist* view and the *federalist* view. The realist view teaches that all of Adam's descendants were *really* present when he sinned. Hence, according to this view, it was not necessary for sin to be transmitted from Adam to his descendants because we were all *really* there somehow when Adam and Eve sinned. The federalist view, on the other hand, teaches that Adam is our representative head. Because Adam represented us, his actions and decisions had a determinative effect on our future.

Let's take a closer look at both of these views, beginning with the realist position.

A key passage of Scripture for the realist position is Hebrews 7:4–9. The author of Hebrews is establishing here that Jesus is a great high priest in a priesthood superior to the Levitical priesthood. To make his point, he argues that when Abraham paid tithes to Melchizedek, Levi was in Abraham's loins so that, in a manner of speaking, Levi was present and tithed to Melchizedek, thereby demonstrating the superiority of Melchizedek's priesthood over the Levitical priesthood (Hebrews 7:4–10). The realist explanation for the transmission of original sin submits, then, that all of Adam's descendants were *really* present when Adam sinned, just as Levi was "present" when Abraham paid tithes to Melchizedek.

Now if you feel a headache coming on as you try to understand the realist position, it may help to think of the image of a tree with roots and branches. This was a picture used by Jonathan Edwards, who defended a variation of the realist position: "And though [God] dealt more immediately with Adam, yet it was as the *head* of the whole body, and the *root* of the whole tree; and in his proceedings with him, he dealt with all the branches as if they had been existing in their root."[11] So the realist view argues that all of humanity is vitally and organically one with Adam.

Critics of the realist position object that this view does not offer enough of an explanation about precisely how we are organically connected to Adam. Further, they contend that too much weight is placed on the Hebrews 7 passage in which Levi paid tithes to Melchizedek.[12] They point out that the author of Hebrews was not intending to teach us how sin was transmitted; he was focused on declaring the superiority of Christ as our great high priest.

The second major explanation for the transmission of Adam's sin is called the *federalist* or *covenant* view. This view teaches that Adam is the corporate head of all humanity. The word *federal* comes from the Latin *foedus*, which means "covenant." As our covenant head, when Adam sinned, he did so not only on behalf of himself but also for all those he represented, his future descendants.[13] In support of the federalist view is the fact that it fits nicely with Adam's kingly role in the garden of Eden. The Bible consistently reinforces the idea that the actions of kings have consequences for their people. As mentioned in chapter 1, when King David sinfully took a census, seventy thousand subjects died as a result (2 Samuel 24:15). Repeatedly throughout the Psalms, we see references to the truth that God's appointed king *represents* his people.[14]

Though it may seem somewhat easier to grasp, the federalist view is not without its weaknesses too. Critics object that it strains justice to say that all human beings had solidarity with Adam if the only thing connecting Adam and his descendants is a declaration from God saying that Adam was appointed as their representative. A second criticism of the federalist view is that simply *saying* that Adam was a royal representative does not account for the corruption of the nature of all his descendants. Even if it is conceded that Adam acted as a covenant head and that all are guilty because their representative failed, this does not explain why everyone from Adam on has been born a sinner.

So which of the two views is correct? Which best explains *how* we are roped to Adam? Were we really present when Adam sinned, or should we see Adam as our covenant head who represented us as his descendants? Personally, I am not convinced that the realist and federalist explanations of the transmission of Adam's sin must be mutually exclusive. New Testament scholar Douglas Moo wonders if we need to make a definitive choice between the two explanations.[15] This was also the position of D. Martyn Lloyd-Jones, who (rightly in my opinion) concluded that both the realist and federalist views help us understand different aspects of how Adam's sin was transmitted.[16] While the realist view leaves us with some mystery as to precisely *how* we are united with Adam, our inability to plumb the depth of this truth does not negate the fact that it is true. And though the federalist view rightly emphasizes Adam as our representative covenant head, it needs the balance of the realist position because our union is about more than *just* representation; it is also a vital and organic reality.

If all of this makes you feel lost, tired, and confused, let me suggest you take away three key points from this brief introduction to the doctrine of original sin.

1. All are counted guilty because of Adam's sin.
2. All have a corrupt nature because of Adam's sin. "We sin because we are sinners" rather than "we are sinners because we sin."
3. All the death and suffering and pain of human history are predicated on Adam's failure in the garden.

These three points cover the basics of original sin, and they are statements that all orthodox theologians can agree on. The doctrine of original sin teaches us that when Adam disobeyed God in the garden, he did not act in a private capacity. Rather, all of humanity — you and I included — had solidarity with Adam. To put it another way, when Adam jumped off the cliff of sin and death in his rebellion against God, we were tied to him in his rebellion, and he pulled us over the side with him. We now live in the dark abyss of death, mourning, crying, and pain. The doctrine of original sin is the ultimate *negative* application of the principle of the rope.

It is critical that we know and understand the doctrine of original sin. Yet sadly, even among evangelical Christians, there are few today who know and believe this essential doctrine of our faith. Dorothy Sayers, writing more than fifty years ago, made this discouraging assessment of the doctrinal knowledge of believers in England: "The brutal fact is that in this Christian country not one person in a hundred has the faintest notion of what the Church teaches about God or man or society, or the person of Jesus Christ."[17] Sayers later added, "Needless to say, the whole doctrine of original sin will have to be restated in terms that the ordinary modern man, brought up on biology and Freudian psychology, can understand."[18] If this was true in Sayers's time, it is all the more so today. The doctrine of original sin needs to be taught carefully, and I believe one of the keys to helping people understand this doctrine is the principle of the rope. Grasping the concept of solidarity — how we are bound to others in our good and bad choices — is essential to grasping the eternal implications of Adam's sin and our guilt before God.

This is especially true today because modern thinkers tend to vehemently object to the doctrine of original sin, more so to than any other doctrine. Alan Jacobs relates:

> Of all the religious teachings I know, none — not even the belief that some people are eternally damned — generates as much hostility as the Christian doctrine we call "original sin."
> It is one of the most "baleful" of ideas says one modern

scholar; it is "repulsive" and "revolting," says another. I have seen it variously described as an insult to the dignity of humanity, an insult to the grace and loving-kindness of God, and an insult to God and humankind alike. And many of those who are particularly angry about the doctrine of original sin are Christians. One of the great evangelists of the nineteenth century, Charles Finney, called the doctrine "subversive of the gospel, and repulsive to human intelligence." A hundred years earlier an English minister, John Taylor of Norwich had cried, "What a God he must be, who can curse his innocent creatures before they have a being! Is this thy God, O Christian?"[19]

At this point, you may find yourself inclined to agree with some of these sentiments. Some will say, "It all seems so unfair. I will allow that Scripture teaches that Adam represented all of humanity and that because of his sin, death and suffering and pain entered the world. And there can be no question that there is great evil in the world. But this idea that the sins of one man can be counted against millions and millions of people — it just doesn't seem right." If that's where you're at, bear with me a bit longer. I want to suggest that if the principle of the rope is true, then the bad news is really as bad as you and I make it out to be. It means that despite our best efforts and good intentions, we cannot change the reality of sin in this world or in our lives. Original sin is, indeed, bad news — the very worst sort of news, especially for those of us who have been taught that we can change ourselves, our future, and the world we live in.

The principle of the rope means that the decision that Adam made to rebel against God has left us in a desperate situation. We stand condemned as rebels excluded from God's good future, unless we are saved from our wretched condition.

I won't deny any of this. And that's why you will want to read the next chapter before giving up on this book altogether. Because, as we will see, though the bad news is bad, the good news is far better than any of us could have ever imagined.

CHAPTER THREE

The Rope That Is Stronger

In God's sight there are two men—Adam and Jesus Christ—and these two men have all other men hanging at their girdle strings.

Thomas Goodwin, seventeenth-century president of Magdalen College, Oxford

A way of thinking that makes us aloof to solidarity with Adam makes us [unable to understand] the solidarity by which salvation comes.

John Murray, *Lectures in Systematic Theology*

For as by a man came death, by a man has come also the resurrection of the dead. For as in Adam all die, so also in Christ shall all be made alive.

1 Corinthians 15:21–22

One of the most famous objections against the principle of the rope was lodged by the fictional Ivan Karamazov. If you are a student of literature, you will recall that Ivan Karamazov was one of Fyodor Dostoyevsky's title characters in *The Brothers Karamazov*, a book regarded by many as the greatest novel ever written. Regardless of whether or not you are a fan of Russian literature, Ivan Karamazov's objection to the principle of the rope is one that needs to be considered.

Keep in mind our progress thus far. Chapter 1 set forth the argument that we are bound (or roped) to other people. Others represent us and determine our identity when they make decisions. And each of us represents other people as well. Contra modern individualism, no one person's identity can be understood strictly on an individual level. We have solidarity with one another. This is the principle of the rope.

In chapter 2, we saw that the ultimate negative example of the principle of the rope is the doctrine of original sin, which teaches that because Adam sinned, and because he did so representing all of humanity, then we are born as sinners into an existence where people, including children, suffer.

Now to consider Ivan Karamazov and his case against Christianity. The reason *The Brothers Karamazov* is so highly regarded isn't because it is the quintessential murder mystery, though it is a murder mystery — revolving around the murder of the evil father and the subsequent investigation. Nor is *The Brothers Karamazov* acclaimed because it was written with the soaring prose of Shakespeare. Rather, the greatness of the novel is that in it Dostoyevsky addressed the objections of the modern era against Christianity.

Dostoyevsky knew that to adequately respond to the critiques of Christianity being raised by modern intellectuals, it was first necessary to let them raise their most compelling objections. To that end, Dostoyevsky gave voice to these critiques against Christianity through one of the title characters, a man named Ivan Karamazov. The heart of Ivan Karamazov's case against Christianity is found in two of the most famous chapters of literature ever written. In these chapters, Ivan tells his brother Alyosha, the sensitive younger brother who represents the Christian faith, that he cannot accept a god who allows the suffering of people, particularly little children. Ivan admits that though there are several arguments he can raise against Christianity, the fact that innocent children suffer is sufficient to win his case:

> But then there are [suffering children], and what am I to do about them? That's a question I can't answer. For the hundredth time I repeat, there are numbers of questions, but I've only taken the children, because in their case what I mean is so unanswerably clear. Listen! If all must suffer to pay for the eternal harmony, what have children to do with it, tell me, please? It's beyond all comprehension why they should suffer?[1]

To be sure that his readers knew he was wrestling with real-life questions and not just writing fiction, Dostoyevsky had Ivan use true stories of suffering children taken either from historical sources or the newspapers.[2] *The Brothers Karamazov* was originally published serially in the newspaper, and because the stories of these children were so horrific and true, Dostoyevsky feared his editors would refuse to publish the full accounts, and he pleaded with them not to delete these stories. He rightly understood that the only way to refute the objections was by presenting them in the most authentic and honest way he could.

One of the true stories Dostoyevsky included was that of a young boy fed to the dogs by some army officers, right in front of his mother. Another was a story about the parents who smeared their daughter's face with excrement because she wet her bed. I'll spare you the details. Dostoyevsky includes both of these accounts in his book, and after Ivan recites the account of the little girl, he exclaims, "The whole world of knowledge is not worth the tears of that little child to 'dear God.' I'm not talking about the sufferings of grown-ups, they ate the apple and to hell with them, let the devil take them all."[3]

The question Dostoyevsky is trying to address is one you have likely asked at some point as well: "What is the Christian response to the fact that we live in a world where such evil and horrific things take place?" The fictional Ivan Karamazov anticipates the historic Christian explanation for these things — the doctrine of original sin, the belief that the evil and suffering we see in this world is the result of Adam's disobedience and rebellion against our Creator. And yet he does not find it to be an acceptable answer:

> I understand solidarity in sin among men; solidarity in retribution I also understand; but what solidarity in sin do little children have? And if it is really true that they, too, are in solidarity with their fathers in all the fathers' evildoings, that truth certainly is not of this world and is incomprehensible to me. Some joker will say, perhaps, that in any case the child will grow up and have time enough to sin, but there's this boy who didn't grow up but was torn apart by dogs at the age of eight.[4]

Ivan Karamazov famously concludes that, given the suffering of children, he is inclined to "return my ticket" and reject Christianity.[5]

So what can a Christian say in response to these objections? How can we account for the reality that we live in a world in which all people, including small children, have solidarity with Adam and consequently suffer? For answers, we must turn to the Bible, and in particular to the book of Romans.

The Gospel in Romans 5:12 – 21

The book of Romans is a letter written by the apostle Paul to the church in Rome. It offers a summary of Paul's theological thought, and Romans 5:12 – 21 is the theological center of the entire book. Writing on this passage, Dr. Martyn Lloyd-Jones once characterized it as "undoubtedly the most important section, in a sense, of the whole of this wonderful epistle."[6] To appreciate exactly *why* Romans 5:12 – 21 is so pivotal, we need to consider the context for Paul's letter. When Paul wrote to the young church in Rome, he wanted to speak to a number of real-life challenges the church was facing. Paul sought to address the following:

- the need to raise missions support for a trip to Spain. Paul knew that if churches were planted in Spain, there would be gospel-centered churches across the breadth of the Roman Empire; such missionary work would require support from the church, and the church in Rome was ideally positioned to be a sending church for a trip to Spain (Romans 15:23 – 29)
- divisions in the church in Rome between Jews and Gentiles — even a cursory reading of Romans reveals that Paul repeatedly speaks to tensions between Jewish and Gentile Christians (Romans 1:13 – 17; 2:12 – 29; 9; 11; 14)
- the need to take up a collection for the poor (Romans 15:26 – 32)
- how Christians should deal with divisive people who threaten the unity of believers (Romans 16:17)

- pride regarding spiritual gifts that threatened to create divisions (Romans 12:3 – 8)
- the reality that Christians are engaged in a spiritual war (Romans 16:20)
- how Christians should view their relationship with the Roman Empire (Romans 13:1 – 7)

Though the list of problems in the letter to the Romans is rather long, the solution to all of them is simple and clear: the *gospel*. Paul knew that if his readers got the good news about Jesus Christ right, then everything else would fall into place. Paul's central aim throughout Romans is to show why the gospel is the greatest news ever proclaimed. From the opening verses, Paul makes his thesis clear.

> I am not ashamed of the gospel, for it is the power of God for salvation to everyone who believes, to the Jew first and also to the Greek. For in it the righteousness of God is revealed from faith for faith, as it is written, "The righteous shall live by faith."
>
> Romans 1:16 – 17

When we arrive at Romans 5:12 – 21, we come to the very heart of Paul's gospel presentation. In this section, Paul explains how there can be victory in Christ. He begins by reminding his readers of the doctrine of original sin:

> Therefore, just as sin came into the world through one man, and death through sin, and so death spread to all men because all sinned —
>
> Romans 5:12

Paul says that the reason things have gotten so sinfully crazy in this world is because of the actions of one person — Adam. As we saw in the last chapter when we looked at the doctrine of original sin, when Adam jumped off the cliff of rebellion against God, he pulled us with him over the edge into sin and death.

Thankfully, Paul does not end with Adam's failure. Even as Paul reminds his readers of the doctrine of original sin and of our solidarity with Adam, he moves on to announce a parallel truth. Just as we have been united to Adam — roped to him in his sin and rebellion — so now we can be united to Christ — roped to him — and receive his freedom, forgiveness, and salvation from our sin.

> For as by the one man's disobedience the many were made sinners, so by the one man's obedience the many will be made righteous.
>
> Romans 5:19

Take a breath for a moment and stop to consider Paul's words. By the One (Christ) many can be made righteous. In other words, though we are all roped to Adam in a negative way, it is now possible for us to be roped to the Lord Jesus Christ in a positive way. For all who are lost in the mire of this sinful world because of Adam's sin, Christ now throws a lifeline to rescue us. He severs our tie to Adam and binds us to himself.

It is critical to note that Paul is not suggesting we are now roped to *both* Adam and Christ. If this were true, we would be left bound by two ropes, caught in a figurative tug-of-war between Christ and Adam. Instead, Paul says in Romans 5:12 – 21 that being roped to Christ is superior to our death in Adam. The cross cancels our solidarity with Adam and links us to Christ. Note how the words of contrast are emphasized below so you can see how Paul is repeatedly making this crucial point in this passage:

> Therefore, just as sin came into the world through one man, and death through sin, and so death spread to all men because all sinned — for sin indeed was in the world before the law was given, but sin is not counted where there is no law. Yet death reigned from Adam to Moses, even over those whose sinning was not like the transgression of Adam, who was a type of the one who was to come.

But the free gift **is not like** the trespass. For if many died through one man's trespass, **much more** have the grace of God and the free gift by the grace of that one man Jesus Christ abounded for many. And the **free gift is not like the result of that one man's sin**. For the judgment following one trespass brought condemnation, **but** the free gift following many trespasses brought justification. For if, because of one man's trespass, death reigned through that one man, **much more** will those who receive the abundance of grace and the free gift of righteousness reign in life through the one man Jesus Christ.

Therefore, as one trespass led to condemnation for all men, so one act of righteousness leads to justification and life for all men. For as by the one man's disobedience the many were made sinners, so by the one man's obedience the many will be made righteous. Now the law came in to increase the trespass, but where sin increased, **grace abounded all the more**, so that, as sin reigned in death, grace also might reign through righteousness leading to eternal life through Jesus Christ our Lord.

Douglas Moo beautifully summarizes this by saying that there now exists a life-giving union between Christ and his own that is similar to, but more powerful than, the death-producing union between Adam and those who belong to him.[7]

So what does this mean, practically, for us?

It means that the principle of the rope, though we first experience it as the *worst* possible news, is ultimately *good* news. The principle of the rope is what underlies the good news of the gospel, namely, that if we are roped to Christ, we are so bound to him that nothing — not even the rope that ties us to Adam — can ever separate us from his love.

In the next chapter, I'll unpack more of the implications of this amazing truth, but for now, I want to address the question we began with: How does this address the suffering of children?

Why does God allow this evil? As we have seen, the reality of solidarity—what we have called the principle of the rope—means that God takes the decisions and choices we make very seriously, and he does not treat us simply as individuals when we make these decisions. This means that our solidarity is both bad and good news. Negatively, we live in a world that is fallen and corrupt because of the sin of one man. Great evil exists in this world because we are evil. Children suffer because this world we live in is cursed and fallen, and it is inhabited by people living in rebellion against their Creator. We are foolish to deny this, despite the protests of those like Ivan Karamazov. And yet, this truth is what makes the gospel such good news. The very principle that condemns us also gives us great hope. Because God has made us and this world to operate on a principle of solidarity, there is hope that we can be saved from the consequences of Adam's sin, not by our own efforts (which can never suffice), but through the actions of a representative, someone who will do what we cannot do, someone who will suffer in our place, on our behalf.

The good news of solidarity is what empowers the gospel, making it effectual in our lives. Just as Adam sinned, condemning us to death, in Christ we can be raised. In the timeless words of Charles Wesley:

> No condemnation now I dread: Jesus, and all in Him, is
>   mine!
> Alive in Him, my living Head, And clothed in righteousness
>   divine,
> Bold I approach th'eternal throne, And claim the crown,
>   through Christ my own.[8]

CHAPTER FOUR

Bound to a New King

Union with Christ is as real as though there were in fact a literal umbilical cord uniting them, leading "all the way" from Christ in heaven to the believer on earth.

Robert L. Reymond, *A New Systematic Theology of the Christian Faith*

Any attack even on the least of men is an attack on Christ, who took the form of man, and in his own Person restored the image of God in all that bears communion with the form. Through fellowship and communion with the incarnate Lord, we recover our true humanity, and at the same time we are delivered from that individualism which is the consequence of sin, and retrieve our solidarity with the whole human race.

Dietrich Bonhoeffer, *The Cost of Discipleship*

"The glory that you have given me I have given to them, that they may be one even as we are one."

John 17:22

Thus far I have referred to identification with Christ with the picture of a rope binding us to Christ. But at this point we need to move to more precise theological language. Theologians refer to solidarity with Christ as "union with Christ." The importance of this doctrine cannot be overstated. John Calvin wrote that union with Christ is a matter of "the highest degree of importance,"[1] and theologian John Murray has said that "union with Christ is ... the central truth of the whole doctrine of salvation ... It is not simply a phase of the application of redemption; it underlies every aspect of redemption."[2] Robert Letham, in the introduction to his splendid book on union with Christ, writes, "Union with Christ is right at the center of the Christian doctrine of salvation."[3]

Union with Christ means that God sees the believer and Christ as *one*. This reality underlies the message of the gospel and affects every aspect of our salvation. Because Christ is righteous, the believer is righteous. Because Christ is the child of God, the believer is God's child. Because Christ is eternally blessed, the believer is eternally blessed. Union with Christ means that a believer is *in* Christ and Christ is *in* the believer, who is being increasingly conformed to the image of Christ. For those who belong to Christ, the final hope and promise is that one day soon, we will be in the presence of Christ for all of eternity.

The Westminster Longer Catechism, Q. 66, defines "union with Christ" as "the work of God's grace, whereby [believers] are spiritually and mystically, yet really and inseparably, joined to

Christ as their head and husband; which is done in their effectual calling."

Let's consider this definition phrase by phrase. Union with Christ is first defined as "the work of God's grace." In other words, we are united to Christ not because we deserve anything or have earned something from God, but only because God has intervened on our behalf (Ephesians 2:1 – 10; Titus 3:3 – 8). Christ, along with his blessings, his righteousness, and his identity, is given to us, undeserved and unmerited.

The catechism goes on to say that believers are united with Christ "spiritually." This refers to the reality that this union is accomplished by the work of the Holy Spirit. It is only through the work of the Holy Spirit that believers can partake of Christ. John Murray writes about this: "It is union of an intensely spiritual character consonant with the nature and work of the Holy Spirit so that in a real way surpassing our power of analysis Christ dwells in his people and his people dwell in him."[4] This is a union that, first, determines our legal status with Christ as our representative head and, second, that revives and sustains us by the work of the Holy Spirit.[5]

The Westminster definition also says that believers are united with Christ "mysteriously." The word *mysteriously* is used by theologians differently from the way it would be used in a Sherlock Holmes novel. A mystery is "something which eye hath not seen nor ear heard neither hath entered the heart of man but which God has revealed unto us by his Spirit and which by revelation and faith comes to be known and appropriated by men."[6] Unlike the mysteries solved by Sherlock, our union with Christ is not something we must figure out or deduce using our human wisdom. We know it only because God has made it known to us through His Word. It has been *revealed*.

Along with understanding our union with Christ, it is helpful to know that there are two opposite errors we must guard against.

On the one hand, union with Christ does not involve a confusion of the identity of believers with Christ. Abraham Kuyper clarifies this when he writes, regarding union with Christ, "This may not be understood as obliterating the boundary between the divine nature and the human."[7] On the other hand, our union with Christ is something more substantial than a mere *association* of distinct individuals, as you would find in a human society.[8]

Lest you think all this discussion of doctrine is sounding a bit academic, let me assure you that the doctrine of union with Christ is of utmost relevance for life. Regularly as a pastor I spend time with people who have been flattened by tragedy. As I think back over the last twenty years of ministry, I can remember the time a young father died suddenly of a heart attack, and it was my job to take his little girl home from camp. Or as long as I live I will never forget being with parents when they learned that a child had been killed, or being with those who looked through the window at the morgue to identify their son, or sharing tears in the emergency room with people in our church. I have pleaded with couples not to get a divorce, and then seen one of the spouses walk away with someone else. I've talked many times with people who were being sucked under in the quicksand of depression. And in every one of those pastoral situations, with cancer, divorce, death, depression, every time I walk up the steps to stand behind the pulpit, I go with the premise that I can assure people the Lord Jesus Christ has relevance for their tragedy today. How can that be? How can it be for a mother, sobbing, weeping, devastated at the morgue, that a pastor can say, "Rest in Christ. Lean on him. Be still and know that he is God." And the answer to this question of why something as remote as Calvary can be significant for today is because of union with Christ. For those who believe, his righteousness, his perfection, his beauty, his glory, his awesomeness, his victory, his resurrection — none of these are far away. God is not watching us from a distance. If you have bowed your knee to the Son, then you are identified with him; by the work of the Holy Spirit you have been united with him. And for those who know Christ, there is *nothing* remote about what he has done.

Images of Union with Christ

Scripture gives us a plurality of images to help us see how the believer is united to Christ. None of these pictures *exhaustively* explain this union. Taken individually, they each have limitations, but considered together they deepen our understanding of the wonderful truth that we are united to our Lord, Savior, and King.

One of the first illustrations of union we find in the Bible is the image of a building — the temple. In this illustration, Christians are seen as being united to Christ in a manner similar to the way the stones of a building are mortared to the cornerstone. Both Paul and Peter illustrate union with Christ in this way. Paul writes to the Ephesians:

> So then you are no longer strangers and aliens, but you are fellow citizens with the saints and members of the household of God, built on the foundation of the apostles and prophets, Christ Jesus himself being the cornerstone, in whom the whole structure, being joined together, grows into a holy temple in the Lord. In him you also are being built together into a dwelling place for God by the Spirit.
>
> Ephesians 2:19 – 22

Peter also encourages his readers by telling them that they are like "living stones" placed together to be the temple of God.

> As you come to him, a living stone rejected by men but in the sight of God chosen and precious, you yourselves like living stones are being built up as a spiritual house, to be a holy priesthood, to offer spiritual sacrifices acceptable to God through Jesus Christ.
>
> 1 Peter 2:4 – 5

In addition to the imagery of building, the apostle Paul also uses the analogy of the physical body to illustrate how we are vitally united to Christ:

> Rather, speaking the truth in love, we are to grow up in every way into him who is the head, into Christ, from whom the whole body, joined and held together by every joint with which it is equipped, when each part is working properly, makes the body grow so that it builds itself up in love.
>
> Ephesians 4:15 – 16

Paul tells us that we are connected to Christ as a part of his body. If you don't mind experiencing a bit of pain for the next few weeks, you can try this simple exercise to aid you in grasping just how vital it is to be united this way. Go to your kitchen and open the silverware drawer as far as it will go. Place the finger of your nonwriting hand just inside the wood that frames your drawer. Now, slam the drawer as hard as you can. I am warning you in advance that this will be painful, so you may want to hold your breath. If you are foolish enough to take my advice (which I am not recommending at all), you will soon discover that your finger is going to be sore for several days. It may never be quite the same, depending on how much damage you do. My point in suggesting this morbid exercise is this: Having slammed your finger in the drawer, would you say that your finger is a part of you, vitally connected to your body? Was the pain you experienced limited to your finger, or did it affect your entire being — other parts of your body as well?

You get the idea. Scripture teaches that those who belong to Christ, who trust in him by faith, are united to him as intimately as a finger belongs to the body. Paul tells us that we, together, are the body and Christ is our head. Because of this, we need never fear condemnation. Spurgeon paints this picture with vivid detail: "So long as a man's head is above water you cannot drown his feet and as long as Christ, the Head of the mystical body, rises above the torrent of condemnation, there is no condemning even the least and feeblest member of His body!"[9] Our union with Christ means that our salvation is secure. Because he is victorious, we share in his victory and in the benefits of salvation.

We are given yet another image of union by Jesus himself. In the upper room, Jesus compared our union with him to the connection of branches to a vine (John 15:1 – 17). Jesus assured his disciples that if we abide in him, we will continue to bear fruit. Lacking this vital union with him means that our lives lack life and will fail to bear fruit. Those who are not united to Christ will be thrown away, like a branch that is gathered and thrown into the fire (John 15:7). This organic image of the vine reminds us that our union with Christ is a vital source of spiritual life for believers. Apart from a real, spiritual union with Christ, believers lack the spiritual "food" they need to survive. Our vitality — our spiritual life and health — is dependent on our being united to Christ.

Two additional images speak to another aspect of union — relational intimacy. In Ephesians 5:22 – 33, Paul compares Christ's relationship with the church to the conjugal and spiritual union of marriage in which a man and a woman become one flesh. The metaphor of marriage reminds us yet again that our personality and uniqueness as individual believers are not mixed or confused with Christ in this union. No human relationship is more intimate than marriage, yet both the bride and groom, while experiencing a union of their persons and a shared identity, still retain their uniqueness as individuals. And yet the relationship of marriage is an intimate one in which two lives are inseparably intertwined and interconnected. In a fallen world, marital intimacy can be one of the greatest sources of joy and pain that we know with another person. Our union with Christ is greater than this marital intimacy, as it is based on a relationship not with another sinner but with our sinless Savior, who has demonstrated his love for us by dying on our behalf.

Another image speaks to this aspect of intimacy as well — our relationship as children of our heavenly Father. Paul in Ephesians 1 tells us that God the Father has determined that believers belong to him *in* Christ, even before the foundation of the world. He goes on to state that those who believe are *adopted* through his glorious grace (Ephesians 1:5). Adoption by the Father *in* Christ speaks to the reality that we become co-heirs together with the eternal Son, as adopted sons and daughters of God. As Paul explains in Romans 8:16 – 17, "we are children of God, and if children, then heirs — heirs of God and fellow heirs with Christ." And so all of the benefits and blessings of sonship, of being a child of our heavenly Father, are now ours through our union with Christ.

Each of these pictures richly illuminates what it means to be united with Christ. But perhaps the most startling picture the Scriptures use to teach us about our union with Christ is through the very relationships within the Godhead — the eternal community of the Father, Son, and Holy Spirit. In John 17, our union with Christ is compared to the intra-Trinitarian relationships of the Godhead. This is the good news that we have been united with the very life of the uncreated God. Read it for yourself.

> [I pray] that they may all be one, just as you, Father, are in me, and I in you, that they also may be in us, so that the world may believe that you have sent me. The glory that you have given me I have given to them, that they may be one even as we are one, I in them and you in me, that they may become perfectly one, so that the world may know that you sent me and loved them even as you loved me.
>
> John 17:21 – 23

In this amazing passage, Jesus prays that he and his people "may all be one, just as you, Father, are in me, and I in you." He goes on to say, "that they may be one even as we are one." John Murray, commenting on this passage, found it staggering that our union with Christ would be compared to the eternal union of persons existing in the Godhead.[10] But this is, in fact, the good news of the gospel. Understanding the significance of this is foundational to our grasp of the purpose and work of Christ. The doctrine of the Trinity gives us a glimpse into the very nature of God, the ever-giving and ever-loving nature that is at the heart of his self-identity. And looking at the union of the Godhead helps us better understand our own union with Christ — how we can be one and yet distinct.[11] Robert Letham explains:

> Indeed, the Christian faith can be summed up as, inter alia, a series of unions. There is the union of the three persons in the Trinity, the union of the Son of God with our human nature, the union of Christ with his church, the union established by the Holy Spirit with us as he indwells us. Each of these unions preserves the integrity of the constituent elements or members, being at once a real union and simultaneously not absorbing the one into the other.[12]

As we've seen, the principle of the rope is an undeniable aspect of life. Without obliterating our identity as individuals (as we will see in the next chapter), we are yet counted as *one* with others. Our lives are bound together, and we are directly affected by others' choices and actions. It is easy to focus on the negative aspects of our solidarity — our union with Adam in original sin and the suffering we see in this world — because our lives continue to be affected by the evil choices of sinful men and women. Yet we need to grasp that the reality of solidarity makes possible the good news of our union with Christ. Because of the principle of the rope, we can be united to Christ. All of the benefits and blessings that he has merited by his righteous life, atoning death, victorious resurrection, and glorious ascension to heaven are now ours through the grace of God. Ultimately, it is our union with Christ that makes possible the greatest miracle of all — our inclusion into the very life of God, the inner relationships of the Trinity. Counted in the Son, adopted by the Father, and indwelt by the Spirit, we experience the fullness of love because of our solidarity with Jesus. The principle of the rope makes the good news true for you and me.

When confronted with the reality of evil, the death of innocent children and suffering that we cannot explain or even comprehend, the most important thing we can do in response is fly as quickly as possible to the good news of our union with Christ. We can acknowledge the reality of sin and evil, as the Scriptures do, by pointing to the truth that we stand condemned, that we are under the curse, because of the rebellion of Adam. But the very reality that condemns us is also the basis of the good news that God graciously announces to us — that we can be cut off from Adam and united to Christ. This is essentially what Martyn Lloyd-Jones preached in response to those who questioned the doctrine of original sin: "Once more I repeat what I said previously, that we must not begin to question our relationship to the world's first man, Adam, because every time you put the question I will make you ask the same question about our relationship to the Lord Jesus Christ."[13]

As you can see, solidarity — the principle of the rope — is simply an aspect of the world that God has created. It is fundamental. It is something we can try to deny, but like gravity we must live with it, whether we like it or not, each and every day. But we can do more than merely *accept* it as true; we can revel in this truth, knowing that through our identification with Christ and our union with Him, we have hope for the future. Though the storms of life threaten to drown us and destroy us, we can truly say that it is well with our souls because we have put our faith and trust in King Jesus. Through Jesus, God has extended to you the rope of salvation, and when you are roped to him, you will be saved.

The rope of the gospel is stronger than the rope of original sin.

CHAPTER FIVE

Can We Blame the Rope?

There is also the institution of the individual, and to dis-
count our individuality is to desecrate our responsible relations to God and to men. The principle of solidarity can be
exaggerated; it can become an obsession and lead to fatal-
istic abuse (cf. Ezekiel 18:2). All such exaggeration is evil.

John Murray, *The Imputation of Adam's Sin*

His disciples asked him, "Rabbi, who sinned, this man or
his parents, that he was born blind?"

John 9:2

"As I live, declares the Lord GOD, this proverb shall no
more be used by you in Israel. Behold, all souls are mine;
the soul of the father as well as the soul of the son is mine:
the soul who sins shall die."

Ezekiel 18:3−4

Whose fault was it that country music singer Hank Williams Jr. plunged downward into alcoholism and substance abuse? Was it inevitable that the apple wouldn't fall far from the tree? Answering that question has implications not only for how we listen (or don't listen) to country music, but also for how each of us sees his or her connection to the sins of our family.

Thus far, we have established that God does *not* simply treat us as individuals. The choices and decisions that people make affect the lives of others. If a husband cheats on his wife, it will have disastrous consequences not only for himself but for his family as well. If a political leader declares war, millions of people may die. The actions of people who live near us, the way they choose to care for the land and the resources we share with them, will directly affect our own health and livelihood, even affecting the future of generations yet to come. In some cases, the choices of certain individuals may even affect our eternal future.

There is no denying that there is a principle of solidarity at work in the world. This reality, that we are bound together, that we are more than the product of our individual choices, can be verified in both the Word of God and our own experience. But does this mean we are doomed by the sins of others? Can we use the sins of someone else as an excuse?

Hank Williams Jr. thought he could make a case that he was destined to follow his father into both fame and failure. He certainly did inherit a legacy of both success in show business and substance abuse. The older Williams blazed onto the country music scene at a young age, and by the age of twenty-six he was performing at the Grand Ole Opry. He sang eleven number one hits, had numerous top ten hits, and was a key influence for later stars like Elvis Presley and Bob Dylan. Country Music Television ranked him second only to Johnny Cash on their list of the "40 Greatest Men of Country Music."

Yet as quickly as Hank Sr.'s meteor streaked into the country music atmosphere, he flamed out. The Grand Ole Opry fired him for habitual drunkenness after only three years. His drug and alcohol abuse increased. His wife divorced him, and his life spiraled downward. On December 31, 1952, Hank Sr. hired a college student to drive him to a concert in West Virginia. He drank during the first leg of the journey, and upon arriving at a Knoxville hotel, he had a doctor give him a vitamin B-12 injection laced with morphine to ease his chronic back pain. William's heart stopped, and he died in the backseat of a Cadillac on New Year's Eve 1953 at the age of twenty-nine.

Hank Jr. started even earlier than his father. He began performing at the Grand Old Opry at the age of eight and signed a major recording contract by the time he was fifteen. But along with fame came the opportunities his father had faced — the temptation to turn to drugs and alcohol. Like his father, the son went into a tailspin, and at the age of twenty-three, he attempted suicide. Shortly thereafter, he nearly died in a mountain climbing accident in Montana.

Hank Jr.'s life somewhat stabilized after the accident in 1975. But his struggles with addictions were so legendary that he was eventually compelled to defend himself. In his hit song "Family Tradition," Williams used his own version of the principle of the rope to rationalize that his addictions were inevitable, given the legacy of his father. Williams sang, "If I get stoned and sing all night long, I'm just carryin' on an old family tradition."

Hank Jr. didn't cite any Scripture while singing "Family Tradition," but after reading the first four chapters of this book, you might think he had a case for attributing his addictions to his father. After all, even the Ten Commandments say that the sins of the fathers are visited on the children (Exodus 20:5). So the question is, "Were Hank Jr.'s failures inevitable?"

This is a question we all face. We are all roped in one way or another to various sins that characterize our immediate and extended families. Some people are roped to alcoholism; other families are bound to brokenness in marriage, with a family history riddled with divorce, addictions to pornography, and gambling. We live in a fallen world, and we have solidarity with sinners — most notably our own mothers and fathers and our brothers and sisters.

Given the reality that we are bound together, two obvious questions surface:

1. Is it inevitable that some people will follow in the footsteps of their forefathers? Are some destined to be alcoholics, while others will, of deterministic necessity, end up battling violent tempers?
2. Can we blame our family members for our own sins? For instance, does the fact that an individual struggles with substance abuse make him a victim of his father's choices to be an addict? Does the principle of the rope excuse sin, taking away our responsibility for our own choices in life?

To answer the question of whether or not we can blame our sins on people to whom we are roped, we turn to Ezekiel 18, where precisely this question is in view.

Ezekiel's Response

Some 2,600 years before Hank Williams Jr. explained that he got stoned and sang all night long because of a family tradition, Israel was singing an earlier version of the same song. In Ezekiel 18, we find the Lord's response to Israel's excuse making, given through the prophet Ezekiel. But before we consider Ezekiel's response, we need to first review Israel's desperate situation during the time when Ezekiel prophesied.

Ezekiel the prophet was born in 622 BC, a century after the Northern Kingdom of Israel had fallen to the Assyrians. Around the time Ezekiel was born, a young king named Josiah began instituting reforms, calling the people back to God (2 Kings 23). Though Josiah's reforms were outwardly impressive, there is little evidence that they led to true repentance — a turning of the hearts of the nation back to the ways of God.[1]

Josiah's reign tragically ended when he was killed in battle with the Egyptians, and by 605, the capital city of Jerusalem was under Babylonian control. Eventually, the Babylonians installed a puppet government, deporting the royal family and other key leaders, including Ezekiel, now a young priest trainee, to Babylon. In a matter of months, Ezekiel found himself hundreds of miles from home, living in a foreign land, grieving the loss of his homeland.

The exiled Israelites were not just blaming the Babylonians. Many of them looked to the past and blamed their situation on the decisions and choices their forefathers had made. They even composed a mocking song about their plight: "The fathers have eaten sour grapes, and the children's teeth are set on edge" (Ezekiel 18:2). Not likely to be in the Top 40 today, it climbed the charts in Babylon and was quite popular back in Jerusalem as well (Jeremiah 31:29 – 30). The point of this uninspired proverb was obvious: "We have a bad taste in our mouths because of the poor choices of the previous generation."

This sense of being a victim, and the pattern of shifting blame onto others, quickly led to apathy among the people. Discouraged, many were inclined to dive even further into sin, refusing to take personal responsibility for their future. You can almost hear them saying to one another, "Forget it, man. It doesn't matter what we do now. Our ancestors blew it." The people were cynical and questioned the promises of God. How could God be just, good, and faithful if his people were now in such a miserable condition because of the sins of their forefathers?

Lest you think this cynicism is limited to the ancient Israelites, let me encourage you to consider our own culture today. Often, as a pastor, I hear people caught in sin blame their personal decisions on the sins of their parents. "If only I would have had a different relationship with my mother. She was an angry woman, and I just cannot get past it." Others will blame their fathers. "I was a great football player. Yet my father never made the effort to go to even one of my games, and that is why I turned to alcohol."

While I will grant that there is often truth in what is being shared, *when taken too far*, acknowledging that our lives are affected by the choices of those we are bound to can lead to cynicism, irreverence, apathy, and even bitterness. A pervasive tendency to blame other people for his or her problems invades every area of a person's life. It's a form of spiritual cancer that is far more deadly than any physical cancer. Left untreated, it leads to a victim mentality and spiritual death.

Thankfully, the word God gave to Ezekiel to balance the deluded perspective of the exiled Israelites can inform our own understanding of sin and provide the necessary balance between the principle of the rope and our own personal responsibility. God responded emphatically to the excuses of the deported Israelites:

> "What do you mean by repeating this proverb concerning the land of Israel, 'The fathers have eaten sour grapes, and the children's teeth are set on edge'? As I live, declares the Lord GOD, this proverb shall no more be used by you in Israel. Behold, all souls are mine; the soul of the father as well as the soul of the son is mine: *the soul who sins shall die.*"
>
> Ezekiel 18:2 – 4, emphasis added

In case you missed it, the Lord's point is clear: we cannot blame our sins on the choices and actions of other people. That is not how God's justice works. There will be no more singing of blame-shifting songs. According to God, no generation is limited by the moral decisions of another generation.[2]

God's clear and emphatic command alone should have been enough for his people to accept the matter. But just in case there was some lingering confusion, Ezekiel went on to lay out a number of examples to make his point clear. I've summarized these in the table below:

In each of these three examples, the point is the same: "the soul who sins shall die" (Ezekiel 18:4). The truth is that each generation has a choice to make. Those who follow Christ will be blessed. But those who walk in the way of sinners and sit in the seat of mockers will be like chaff that the wind blows away (Psalm 1). Don't excuse yourself by saying that you are only carrying out a family tradition. Don't complain that you have a bad taste in your mouth because your fathers snacked on sour grapes.

So Is the Principle of the Rope Real?

I realize that at this point some of you will object. I have spent a lot of time in this book arguing that the principle of the rope is real. If this principle is true, and we have solidarity with our ancestors, then why is each generation held responsible? Was it not true that Israel was exiled because their forefathers broke covenant with God? As Jeremiah lamented, "Our fathers sinned, and are no more; and we bear their iniquities" (Lamentations 5:7).

And what about the promise in the Ten Commandments where the Israelites are warned that God is a jealous God, "visiting the iniquity of the fathers on the children to the third and the fourth generation of those who hate me" (Exodus 20:5)? How can

Generation	Text from Ezekiel (emphasis added)
Generation #1 — A righteous man who lives (Ezekiel 18:5–9)	"If a man is righteous and does what is just and right — if he does not eat upon the mountains or lift up his eyes to the idols of the house of Israel, does not defile his neighbor's wife or approach a woman in her time of menstrual impurity, does not oppress anyone, but restores to the debtor his pledge, commits no robbery, gives his bread to the hungry and covers the naked with a garment, does not lend at interest or take any profit, withholds his hand from injustice, executes true justice between man and man, walks in my statutes, and keeps my rules by acting faithfully — *he is righteous; he shall surely live, declares the Lord God.*"
Generation #2 — An evil son who dies (Ezekiel 18:10–13)	"If he fathers a son who is violent, a shedder of blood, who does any of these things (though he himself did none of these things), who even eats upon the mountains, defiles his neighbor's wife, oppresses the poor and needy, commits robbery, does not restore the pledge, lifts up his eyes to the idols, commits abomination, lends at interest, and takes profit; shall he then live? He shall not live. *He has done all these abominations; he shall surely die; his blood shall be upon himself.*"
Generation #3 — A righteous grandson who lives (Ezekiel 18:14–18)	"Now suppose this man fathers a son who sees all the sins that his father has done; he sees, and does not do likewise: he does not eat upon the mountains or lift up his eyes to the idols of the house of Israel, does not defile his neighbor's wife, does not oppress anyone, exacts no pledge, commits no robbery, but gives his bread to the hungry and covers the naked with a garment, withholds his hand from iniquity, takes no interest or profit, obeys my rules, and walks in my statutes; he shall not die for his father's iniquity; *he shall surely live.* As for his father, because he practiced extortion, robbed his brother, and did what is not good among his people, behold, he shall die for his iniquity."

Table 2: Every Generation Has a Choice

the Bible say that iniquity is visited on multiple generations while also insisting that each generation is responsible?

To resolve this tension, some scholars argue that Ezekiel 18 represents a *shift* in biblical thinking. They say that solidarity had been the norm, but when we come to the time of Ezekiel, the prophets had moved beyond this. But this isn't a viable solution for those who believe in the unity of Scripture. Did God somehow change from the time of Moses to the time of Ezekiel? I do not believe that this passage is speaking of a new sort of individualism that replaces our corporate solidarity.[3]

When we encounter these types of tension in Scripture, the best approach is to uphold both truths and seek to understand how they complement one another. Both are true. As we have seen, solidarity is real. Experience and the Bible teach that this is so. For those who decide to reject Christ, their decision has implications not only for themselves but also for those close to them. But this does not mean the people affected have a right to sin.

Let's suppose that I rebel against God and turn my back on my wife and children. There are myriad ways I could do so. Would the consequences of my sin be limited to myself? Of course not! I have solidarity with my family. They would suffer in one way or another, as would the members of the church in which I serve and my friends and neighbors. Since I've authored several books, my decision may even have an effect on those who have read my books. It's hard to know exactly how our choices will work themselves out in the lives of others. Still, my poor decisions would not mean that my wife or children would cease to be responsible for the decisions they make.

The fact that people's sin affects one another was not something that God forgot about when he warned Israel to quit singing their cynical proverbs about fathers sinning and children's teeth being set on edge. Rather, God's point was that while we do have solidarity with others, each of us has a decision to make.

It should also be acknowledged that certain genetic characteristics can be linked to particular sins. Does a genetic predisposition provide an excuse for sinful behavior? Recent studies have indicated that "an abnormally high percentage of boys with a double Y chromosome (XYY) engage in anti-social or criminal behavior."[4] Yet the fact that our genes may make us more susceptible to certain behaviors does not mean we are off the hook. As theologian John Frame cogently argues, genes cannot be an excuse for sin:

> The bottom line, however, is that the genetic element in sin does not excuse it … From a biblical perspective, the difficult fact is that in one sense all sin is inherited. From Adam come both our sin and our misery. We are guilty of Adam's transgression, and from him we ourselves inherit sinful natures. If a genetic predisposition excuses sodomy, then our inheritance from Adam excuses all sin! But that is clearly not the case.[5]

So, in one sense, all of us are genetically predisposed to sin. But the Bible is clear: the fact that we are born sinners does not excuse us. Solidarity with Adam means we are guilty because of Adam's disobedience *and* we suffer the effects of his decision. This means we live in a fallen world, and the disease of sin has been working its way into our bodies, our relationships, and the created world for generations. Its effects are pervasive and thorough.

What hope do we have, then? I would return again to the central argument of this book: the principle of the rope is ultimately *good* news because what Christ accomplished on the cross is more powerful than Adam's rebellion in the garden. This is the recurring message of the Scriptures. Alongside the curse that God promises in the Ten Commandments — that he will bring punishment on those who practice idolatry for several generations — we immediately see the greater promise of God's continued blessing for those who follow him:

> "I, the LORD your God, am a jealous God, punishing the children for the sin of the parents to the third and fourth generation of those who hate me, but *showing love to a thousand generations of those who love me* and keep my commandments."
>
> Exodus 20:5 – 6 NIV, emphasis added

The blessing of God's love is greater than the curse of sin.

The negative and positive applications of the principle of the rope are not symmetrical. Our solidarity in Christ is more powerful than our solidarity in sin with Adam. Knowing this about God, the exiled Israelites need not have played the victim card. The long history of God's mercy toward them should have taught them that sin is never inevitable. God is eager to extend grace in response to repentant hearts.

Turning from Sin to Follow Christ

Ezekiel does not allow God's people to blame their present circumstances on the past. He tells them that the appropriate response, in every generation, is to turn to God in radical repentance. Ezekiel challenges his listeners to repent and choose life, to respond to the mercy of God rather than wallowing in their own justification:

> "Therefore I will judge you, O house of Israel, every one according to his ways, declares the Lord GOD. *Repent and turn from all your transgressions*, lest iniquity be your ruin. Cast away from you all the transgressions that you have committed, and make yourselves a new heart and a new spirit! Why will you die, O house of Israel? For I have no pleasure in the death of anyone, declares the Lord GOD; so turn, and live."
>
> Ezekiel 18:30 – 32, emphasis added

Ezekiel's call for repentance is a stern warning to a generation that had adopted a victim mentality and was caught in the trap of self-justification. And it is a warning we need to hear today. Many Christians today believe in a cheap grace that excuses sin without counting the cost of God's forgiveness in the cross. They falsely assume that God's grace is a license to live for themselves — the very opposite of the biblical gospel. As Paul reminds us in 1 Corinthians 10:1 – 13, there is a form of faith that is superficial. Paul, speaking to the members of the church, reminds them that many of the Israelites who considered themselves the people of God under the old covenant were deceived, thinking they could wear the label without living out what it meant. Paul tells the church that their example was "written down for our instruction" today (1 Corinthians 10:11). He warns them not to presume upon the grace of God. There comes a time when it is too late to turn (Hebrews 12:17), so now — today — is the time to choose life.

There will always be some who will say, "Because of all that has happened in my life, I cannot change. I cannot forgive. I cannot leave behind my old ways. How can God hold me accountable when my life is the result of the sins of others?" If this is where you're at today, let me remind you of Paul's warning to the Corinthians — like Ezekiel's warning to the Israelites in Babylon — not to underestimate the power of God's grace (1 Corinthians 10:13). He reminds them that the sins they face are not exceptional. God always provides a way to escape the bondage of sin, a way to escape the trap of death through faith in Jesus.

We need to remember that the Scriptures, history, and our churches today are filled with people who have responded to the hope of the gospel, despite undergoing great suffering and being roped to the sins of others.

In Scripture, we see Ruth, a Moabite who traced her family lineage to Lot's incestuous relationship with his daughter (Genesis 19:30 – 38). Despite her background, she left her homeland behind and linked herself to an Israelite woman. She became the great-grandmother of Israel's greatest king (other than Jesus), King David.

Daniel was exiled to Babylon, but he followed God in radical obedience, even in a foreign land. He engaged in civil disobedience, even when it meant certain death, and continued to pray with his window open to Jerusalem. Daniel exhibited a faith that will ring for all of eternity and saw the deliverance of God (Daniel 6:19 – 23).

Nehemiah, though he was exiled and experienced suffering because of the sins of others, chose to respond in courage and was used by God to rebuild the walls of Jerusalem.

Or consider Jonathan. If ever anyone was entitled to blame his circumstances on the sins of his father, it would have been Jonathan. Though his father, Saul, had been chosen as king, Saul's disastrous choices cost Jonathan the future throne. Yet Jonathan refused to see himself as a victim. He refused to blame his father or grow angry with God. Instead, this great man of courage and valor (1 Samuel 14:1 – 23) chose to honor the Lord and befriended God's chosen successor to the throne, David, even to the point of risking his own life for him (1 Samuel 18:1 – 5). When there was opportunity for King David to care for Jonathan's crippled son, Mephibosheth, David did not forget his friendship with Jonathan, giving his son a seat at his own table. David's promise reminds us that the actions and decisions of an individual, when they respond in faith to God and not in sin and rebellion, can have a positive effect on generations to come. The rope of the gospel in Jonathan's life proved immeasurably stronger than Saul's sin.

The book of Hebrews gives a list of individuals who made the decision to respond in faith to God rather than seeing themselves as victims of circumstances. Hebrews 11 reminds us of the story of Moses, who "regarded disgrace for the sake of Christ" to have greater value than "the fleeting pleasures of sin" and "the treasures of Egypt" (Hebrews 11:25 – 26). Moses, like the many others mentioned in Hebrews, chose to repent and respond to God in faith — severing their tie with Adam and refusing to embrace the temptations of sin "that so easily entangles" (Hebrews 12:1).

Perhaps you have been pulled down by your family. You have been making all the wrong decisions in your life. Remember, the principle of the rope is not just an idea — it's real. We need to be roped to the Lord Jesus Christ and to his body, the local church. But this isn't something we do for ourselves. God's plan is not to change us as individuals; the principle of the rope means that our union to Christ also unites us to others who are connected to him in faith. As a result of our union, we are mortared into Christian community. The principle of the rope means that God will use the relationships we have with others in the body of Christ to change and transform our lives. God will use our new connection to confront our sinful habits, remind us of truth, and bring healing and victory to our lives. But this can only happen if we are roped into Christian community and involved in a Christ-centered local church. To this topic we now turn as we consider the power of the principle of the rope to effect change in our lives as we embrace our need for Christian community and recognize the importance of the church. It is in the church, more than any other place, that God uses the principle of the rope to apply the benefits of Christ to our lives.

PART 2

APPLYING
THE PRINCIPLE
OF THE ROPE

CHAPTER SIX

Bound Together for Joy

Healthy formation is impossible without a healthy culture embedded within the warp and woof of community ... I would suggest that the concrete manifestations of the shalom offered centrally include faith, hope, and love, for where these are present, so is joy.

James Davison Hunter, *To Change the World*

In the communion of the saints
Is wisdom, safety and delight;
And, when my heart declines and faints,
It's raised by their heat and light.

Richard Baxter

"These things I have spoken to you, that my joy may be in you, and that your joy may be full."

John 15:11

The Bible commands us to be joyful. It's not an option.

How's that joy thing going for you? When you look in the mirror, do you see a joyful person?

I know. It's easier said than done. It's one thing to know we should rejoice, and another to actually do it. There are times when the Christian life can seem very dark. But if you are struggling to rejoice, be encouraged. God doesn't tell us to rejoice without giving us the grace and direction to do so.

The goal of this chapter is to consider from Scripture how we can obey God's command to be joyful. At first, this chapter may feel like a digression from the principle of the rope or the truth of corporate solidarity. Soon enough, you will see how discovering joy is connected with the reality that we are bound together.

I began investigating joy because I realized early on in my pastoral ministry that too many Christians are drifting about in gloomy waters. So I set sail to explore what the Bible teaches about joy. I was looking for a solution to the problem of joy. Why are Christians not rejoicing more? If I had been a Puritan, I would have given the title of my study something like, "An enquiry into an inadequate experience of joy in the life of a Christian, and a proposed biblical solution whereby the Christian faithful can surely and substantially foster more joy in their daily experience." But I am not a Puritan, so I just labeled a file folder, "Joy," hit the books, and made a joy discovery.

In saying that I made a joy discovery, I readily acknowledge that I am like G. K. Chesterton, who, in relationship to Christianity, described himself as "the man who with the utmost daring discovered what had been discovered before."[1] A master of word pictures, Chesterton said he set out to prove the tenets of the modern age. In the end, he was like "the man who landed (armed to the teeth and talking by signs) to plant the British flag on that barbaric temple which turned out to be the Pavilion at Brighton."[2] While looking for something new, Chesterton stumbled upon territory mapped out by Christians for millennia. Thus have I made a discovery about joy. Yet this insight is surely one where Christians need to once again plant a flag.

Three Indisputable Truths Regarding Joy

My first step in studying joy was to properly frame the problem. The problem of joy is a tension that exists between three indisputable truths.

Indisputable truth claim #1: All Christians desire more joy. I have never heard anyone deny he or she wanted happiness or joy. I wouldn't believe someone who did. It is ludicrous to suggest there are people who want to be miserable. Of course, we all agree there are people who make decisions that take them far from joy. Indeed, any honest person would admit to having made multiple decisions that resulted in a loss of joy. Yet, when making those decisions that compromised our joy, our goal was not to be miserable; rather, we chose something against our better judgment because we thought it would bring joy.

Better minds than mine have pointed out that everyone is in pursuit of joy. The great thinker Blaise Pascal summarized:

> All men seek happiness. This is without exception. Whatever different means they employ, they all tend to this end. The cause of some going to war, and of others avoiding it, is the same desire in both, attended with different views. The will

never takes the least step but to this object. This is the motive of every action of every man, even of those who hang themselves.[3]

Indisputable truth claim #2: God wants his people to experience joy. When I assert that God "wants" us to have joy, I am speaking about the moral desire of the Lord in distinction from God's sovereign will. Sovereignly, God always accomplishes his purposes (Romans 8:28). Morally, there are things God wants that do not happen (2 Peter 3:9).

Morally, God wants us to experience joy. Many Scripture references could be cited. Recall how the news of Jesus' birth was announced to shepherds who were keeping watch over their flocks by night: "Fear not, for behold, I bring you *good news of great joy* that will be for all the people. For unto you is born this day in the city of David a Savior, who is Christ the Lord" (Luke 2:10 – 11, emphasis added).

Consider Zechariah's joyous prophecy regarding Jesus' triumphal entry:

> Rejoice greatly, O daughter of Zion!
>   Shout aloud, O daughter of Jerusalem!
> Behold, your king is coming to you;
>   righteous and having salvation is he,
> humble and mounted on a donkey,
>   on a colt, the foal of a donkey.
>
> Zechariah 9:9

As I pointed out at the beginning of this chapter, Scripture commands us to rejoice (Philippians 4:4). So basic is the command for Christians to rejoice that the Westminster Shorter Catechism famously begins with the summary statement that the chief end of humanity is "to glorify God, and to enjoy him forever."

This does not mean in a fallen world that we won't experience times of grief. Indeed, many times when the Bible speaks of joy, it does so while also acknowledging there are times of great sadness (Psalms 30:5, 11 – 12; 126:5; Isaiah 49:13; 61:3; John 16:22; James

1:2 – 3). Joy in the Christian life does not refer to glib happiness. Rather, joy speaks to a deep and abiding pleasure in Christ that withstands the vicissitudes of life and that will one day give way to eternal joy in God's presence (Revelation 21:3 – 5).

Indisputable truth claim #3: The joy level of many Christians is staying in the same place or even diminishing. The reality is that many Christians are not living joyful lives. Too many Christians look as though they reside in Mudville — the setting of the famous American poem, "Casey at the Bat," in which Ernest Lawrence Thayer describes a community that is miserable because their baseball team is in danger of losing. Thayer writes, "So, when Cooney died at second, and Burrows did the same, a pallor wreathed the features of the patrons of the game."

Just in case you've gotten lost in the flowery language, "a pallor wreathed the features of the patrons of the game" means the Mudville fans were so miserable that they looked like they were chewing tinfoil. Later, Thayer adds, "So upon that stricken multitude a deathlike silence sat."

Finally, Casey, mighty Casey, advances to the plate. "Ten thousand eyes were on him as he rubbed his hands with dirt; five thousand tongues applauded when he wiped them on his shirt." Still, things didn't get better even after Mudville's main man advanced to the plate. The poem concludes, "But there is no joy in Mudville — mighty Casey has struck out." Chicago Cubs fans know how they felt.

I bring up the silly poem here to say that Thayer's description of joyless baseball fans fits far too many local congregations. Indeed, one wonders if a church service inspired Thayer to write the poem.

The Problem of Joy

Summarizing our progress to this point, three indisputable truths frame the problem of joy:

1. All Christians desire more joy.
2. God wants his people to experience joy.
3. The joy level of many Christians is staying in the same place or even diminishing.

In my study of joy, when I compared these truth claims, I saw that a tension exists between the first two truths and the third. *If Christians want joy, and God wants us to have joy, how is it that our experience of joy isn't increasing?*

This is the problem of joy, and it is worth thinking about carefully! If we want more joy, and God wants us to be joyful, then I decided it would be necessary to do more biblical study to see how we can follow through on our assignment to rejoice.

Proclaiming the Obvious

Given Paul's direct admonition to the Philippians to rejoice (Philippians 4:4), I continued my study of the joy problem by doing a word study on *joy* in the Pauline letters. In Paul's writings, the Greek word for "joy," *chara*, appears twenty-one times; the main verb, translated "rejoice," *chairō*, is used twenty-nine times.

Meditating on Paul's use of joy words, I first noted the obvious truth that the foundation of all joy is the gospel, or good news, of Christ. When Paul tells the Philippians to rejoice, he says, "Rejoice *in the Lord*." This brings us back to the glorious doctrine of union with Christ. All are born in sin because of their solidarity with Adam. Conversely, those who believe in Jesus have solidarity with the Savior. The good news is that Christ's people are united to him.

William Tyndale gave one of the greatest explanations of why the gospel, the good news, is foundational to joy. Before you criticize his spelling, remember that he wrote this in 1525 — and spelling conventions have changed over the last five hundred years: "Evangelion (that we call the gospell) is a Greek word; and signifieth good, merry, glad and joyful tidings, that maketh a man's heart glad, and maketh him sing, dance, and leap for joy."[4]

To "sing, dance, and leap for joy" must be the response of Christians when we consider that though we were born sinners and by nature were children of wrath (Ephesians 2:1 – 3), if we accept the gift of eternal life, we are no longer condemned. This news will result in celebration. The gospel is the bedrock of joy. And so, when the gospel is diminished, joy is diminished too.

The gospel is diminished, first of all, when professing Christians do not understand the gospel clearly. Jerry Bridges tells the story of how several thousand participants at a Christian convention were surveyed and asked to summarize the gospel. Only one of the respondents gave what could be considered an adequate summary of the gospel.[5] No wonder so many Christians are lacking joy. Every believer must be able to turn to a passage like 1 Corinthians 15:1 – 6 to give a faithful summary of the good news.

The gospel is also diminished — and joy leaks out — when those who have known the gospel for many years lapse into a works mentality in which they think that somehow we must do things to earn God's favor. For this reason, Jerry Bridges reminds us, we must preach the true gospel to ourselves every single day. Otherwise, we will soon feel defeated in the Christian life. Bridges warns:

> You can be sure of one thing, though: When you set yourself to seriously pursue holiness, you will begin to realize what an awful sinner you are. And if you are not firmly rooted in the gospel and have not learned to preach it to yourself every day, you will soon become discouraged and will slack off in your pursuit of holiness.[6]

Finally, a third way in which the gospel is compromised and joy is diminished is that some accept the lie that something other than God will satisfy the desires of their hearts. They become

convinced that if only they made more money, had different relationships, or were married to a different person, then they would
be happier. This is idolatry, and it steals joy. Looking for satisfac-
tion in cheap substitutes is what C. S. Lewis warns against when
he writes that our problem is not that we want too much but that
we want too little:

> We are half-hearted creatures, fooling about with drink and
> sex and ambition when infinite joy is offered us, like an igno-
> rant child who wants to go on making mud pies in a slum
> because he cannot imagine what is meant by the offer of a
> holiday at the sea. We are far too easily pleased.[7]

Beware of cheap substitutes. It is deadly to believe that someone or something other than the Lord Jesus Christ brings joy.
How awful it will be for those who thought they had found the
key to happiness, only to realize that when their life is demanded
of them, they had gotten it completely wrong (Luke 12:20).

The Discovery

So the first thing I confirmed when I began investigating the
problem of joy is that non-gospel thinking diminishes joy. But
grasping that point was only review. I had understood going into
my investigation of the joy problem that the gospel is the foundation of joy.

The question still remained: Why do even Christians, who
know the gospel well, struggle so hard, at a practical level, to
experience joy? I continued to analyze each of Paul's uses of joy
words. What more could I learn about how to increase the experience of joy?

As I persisted in my study of joy in Paul's writings, something
else caught my attention. Before I share my discovery, I'll let you
peruse a number of Paul's uses of joy words to see if you can make
the discovery yourself. Can you identify a trend in what Paul said

brought him joy? Note that I've highlighted the joy words in each passage.

> Your obedience is known to all, so that I *rejoice* over you, but I want you to be wise as to what is good and innocent as to what is evil.
>
> Romans 16:19

> I wrote as I did, so that when I came I might not suffer pain from those who should have made me *rejoice*, for I felt sure of all of you, that my *joy* would be the *joy* of you all.
>
> 2 Corinthians 2:3

> I am acting with great boldness toward you; I have great pride in you; I am filled with comfort. In all our affliction, I am overflowing with *joy*.
>
> 2 Corinthians 7:4

> Therefore we are comforted. And besides our own comfort, we *rejoiced* still more at the *joy* of Titus, because his spirit has been refreshed by you all.
>
> 2 Corinthians 7:13

> I thank my God in all my remembrance of you, always in every prayer of mine for you all making my prayer with *joy*, because of your partnership in the gospel from the first day until now.
>
> Philippians 1:3 – 5

> So if there is any encouragement in Christ, any comfort from love, any participation in the Spirit, any affection and sympathy, complete my *joy* by being of the same mind, having the same love, being in full accord and of one mind.
>
> Philippians 2:1 – 2

> I am the more eager to send him, therefore, that you may *rejoice* at seeing him again, and that I may be less anxious.
>
> Philippians 2:28

Therefore, my brothers, whom I love and long for, my *joy* and crown, stand firm thus in the Lord, my beloved.

Philippians 4:1

What is our hope or *joy* or crown of boasting before our Lord Jesus at his coming? Is it not you? For you are our glory and *joy*.

1 Thessalonians 2:19 – 20

What thanksgiving can we return to God for you, for all the *joy* that we feel for your sake before our God.

1 Thessalonians 3:9

As I remember your tears, I long to see you, that I may be filled with *joy*.

2 Timothy 1:4

I have derived much *joy* and comfort from your love, my brother, because the hearts of the saints have been refreshed through you.

Philemon 7

The trend is easy to spot. In thirty-four of the fifty times *joy* and *rejoice* appear in the Pauline epistles, *Paul connects his experience of joy to his relationship with other believers.* For Paul, the experience of the joy of the gospel took place in shared partnership with other Christians. He did not experience joy as a pious particle. Paul rejoiced as he shared life with other believers. Read 2 Corinthians 2:3 again:

I wrote as I did, so that when I came I might not suffer pain from those who should have made me *rejoice*, for I felt sure of all of you, that my *joy* would be the *joy* of you all.

Paul intertwines his joy with the joy of the Corinthians. The foundation of their joy is the gospel. Yet, Paul's joy wasn't experienced apart from his fellowship with the Corinthians.

Joy is connected to fellowship in many other passages as well. A sampling from John's epistles makes the same point: "That which we have seen and heard we proclaim also to you, so that you too may have fellowship with us; and indeed our fellowship is with the Father and with his Son Jesus Christ. And we are writing these things so that our *joy* may be complete" (1 John 1:3–4, emphasis added).

John knew that the center of what we share together must be Christ. But he also encouraged his readers that in sharing Christ together, their mutual joy would be increased. Elsewhere, he writes, "I *rejoiced* greatly to find some of your children walking in the truth, just as we were commanded by the Father" (2 John 4, emphasis added). And, "I *rejoiced* greatly when the brothers came and testified to your truth, as indeed you are walking in the truth. I have no greater *joy* than to hear that my children are walking in the truth" (3 John 3–4, emphasis added).

Reflecting on how John writes about joy in 1 John, Martyn Lloyd-Jones stressed the connection between fellowship and the experience of joy:

> If there is anything wrong in my relationship to God, I lose fellowship, and I lose the joy. Yes, but if there is anything wrong in my relationship to Christian brothers and sisters, I also lose the joy, and John works this out in a very subtle way. You lose contact with the brethren, and you lose contact with God; you lose your love to God in the same way.[8]

The connection between joy and fellowship is also seen in the Old Testament. Psalm 133 reads:

> Behold, how good and pleasant it is
>   when brothers dwell in unity!
> It is like the precious oil on the head,
>   running down on the beard,
> on the beard of Aaron,
>   running down on the collar of his robes!
> It is like the dew of Hermon,
>   which falls on the mountains of Zion!

For there the LORD has commanded the blessing,
life forevermore.

This psalm reminds us of the sweetness of unity for God's people. David sings that unity is *good* — delicious, sweet, pure, clean, cheerful, and happy. And it is *pleasant* — beautiful, lovely. Unity is a perfect temperature and pure sunshine. David goes on to give us two pictures that illustrate how wonderful it is to be unified. The first is a picture of an anointing ("precious oil on the head"), teaching us that unified believers are lavishly commissioned. A unified church is set apart to do God's work in a special way. And in the second picture, David uses the simile of water (the "dew of Hermon"). Now remember, water was a very precious commodity in that day. The point is that if we are unified, then we will be blessed and refreshed by God — we will be full of joy.

Making the Connection between Joy and Corporate Solidarity

The images of union with Christ help us understand why joy depends on our sharing life with other believers. Mentally review these images. Christians are a *body*, with Christ as our head. Christians are *bricks* mortared into a building, with Christ as the chief cornerstone. These metaphors teach that our connection with Christ necessarily involves connections with other believers. All of us are bound together. We cannot rejoice by ourselves.

One of the most vivid descriptions of being bound together in Christ is found in John 15, where Jesus declares, "I am the vine." By using the picture of a vine and branches, Jesus shows the intimacy of our union with him and with each other. Our union with Christ is more than just a "legal" matter; it is also a vital, spiritual, organic connection.[9] When we abide in Christ, we are connected in such a way that as we are connected *together* with other believers, our lives produce fruit that glorifies God the Father (John 15:8) and increases our joy.

Meditate further on the image of bearing fruit. When I was seven years old, my parents bought a farm. The farm was not yet turning a profit, so my father worked nights at an ammunition plant fifty miles away and then farmed during the day. To this day, I am not sure when he slept! I was the second of six children, and there were plenty of mouths to feed. Even with my dad working two jobs, money was very tight. That summer after we moved to our farm, we discovered an apple orchard on our new property and saw that it was full of good fruit. We were so excited. It was like finding buried treasure. We pulled the apples right off the tree. We picked them off the ground so none would be wasted. My mom baked apple pie, apple cake, apple crisp, apple butter, and apple betty. The smell of apples and cinnamon filled our home.

Even as we inhaled apples, our family sang the praises of our orchard to anyone who would listen. We took our family and friends up the hill and gave them tours of the fruit trees and marveled with them at the trees bending under the weight of so many apples. We "glorified" the trees, even as we thanked God for them.

It is this way with the body of Christ. All over the world, there are believers abiding in Christ. And as Christians abide in Christ, they bear fruit and bring glory to the Father. Space doesn't permit me to describe the ways I've seen this glorified fruit, just in the modestly sized local church in rural Illinois where I serve as pastor. People teach children, lead worship, care for our facilities, serve people at funeral luncheons, study the Bible together, and visit one another in the hospital. Our fruit trees are heavy laden, and they bear delicious fruit. And yet the true glory of the fruit that is borne is not the wonderful fruit itself. All of the credit goes to our great God, who planted and nourishes the trees. Yet, even as we glorify the Father, we also experience great joy (John 15:11). Find a church where people are abiding in Christ, serving one another, and sharing life, and you will find deep joy. "Behold, how good and pleasant it is when brothers dwell in unity!" (Psalm 133:1).

The experience of mutual joy is wonderful in and of itself. It is even more amazing that we can experience the same phenomena with Christ. When we abide in Jesus and glorify the Father, then we bring Jesus joy. Is that stunning to consider? Do you realize today that if you know Jesus Christ, as you abide in him, you can make Jesus smile?

The answer to the problem of joy is clear. We must not live the Christian life solely as though we have an individual relationship with Christ. Rather, to experience more joy, we must be actively investing in body life. No Christian will experience true joy apart from fellowship in the body of Christ, any more than an amputated finger will be healthy.

Fighting for Joy

Let me return to the question with which I began the chapter: Are you living in obedience to God's command to *rejoice always*? None of us are doing this perfectly. If your joy level is particularly low, then take action to rejoice. Begin by rejoicing *in the Lord*. No matter how long you have been a Christian, review the gospel again. Write out a gospel definition. Read books such as Trevin Wax's *Counterfeit Gospels*, Matt Chandler's *The Explicit Gospel*, and Jerry Bridges's *The Discipline of Grace*. Meditate on grace.

Then with your feet fixed firmly on the gospel of the grace, evaluate how invested you truly are in the body of Christ. Look at your giving to your local church over the last year. Does it indicate that you are sharing life with the body of Christ? Giving does not buy joy. Yet you will not experience joy apart from sharing life with your local church. One of the best indicators of where your heart is is the way in which you invest the resources God has given to you.

Consider the use of your time. Does your calendar show that you are sharing life with other Christians? Are you yielding to the temptation to isolate yourself from other believers. Forsaking the assembly does not bring joy to Christ; it grieves him. But when brothers and sisters live together in unity, God bestows his blessing — even "life forevermore" (Psalm 133).

How are you using the spiritual gifts and abilities that God has given to you? The reason to serve in your local church should not be out of some sort of misguided guilt. Rather, you can be confident that as you share life together in serving the King, you will glorify the Father, bring joy to the Son, and experience true joy yourself. Our experience of Christian joy will grow only to the extent that we grow in active fellowship with the body of Christ.

CHAPTER SEVEN

Bound Together in Marriage

The principle of representation underlies all the basic institutions of God in the world—the family, the church, and the state. In other words, solidarity and corporate relationship is a feature of God's government.

John Murray, *Lectures in Systematic Theology*

The reason, then, why Eve was formed out of one of Adam's ribs is that God meant to ratify such a concord between man and wife in that way, that there would be no bond in this world so tight as that.

John Calvin, *Sermons on the Epistle to the Ephesians*

"A man shall leave his father and mother and hold fast to his wife, and the two shall become one flesh." This mystery is profound, and I am saying that it refers to Christ and the church. However, let each one of you love his wife as himself, and let the wife see that she respects her husband.

Ephesians 5:31–33

What is it about marriage that makes it so lovely? There really should be times when we stop to ponder the wonder and beauty of a man and woman becoming one in marriage.

As a pastor, one of my favorite marriage stories has to do with a couple named Mel and Eleanor. Mel was born in 1919. He attended the same church for most of his life. Around the time he graduated from high school, Mel began dating Eleanor, though she was not yet a Christian. Dating unbelievers is *not* a good idea. Yet in Mel and Eleanor's case, God was gracious. A pastor named Cal Beukema shared the seed of the gospel with young Eleanor. By God's grace, her heart was good soil, and the gospel took root. Eleanor believed. Together, she and Mel raised four pretty daughters. The girls sang together at church, and Mel would cry in his pew while they sang because he was so proud of them.

Yet, life is a vapor, as brief and delicate as a soap bubble. Shortly after I became Mel and Eleanor's pastor, a cancer specialist sat with them to tell them that their fifty-seven years of marriage were coming to an end. Together, this couple had parented, served, and loved. Presumably, they had argued and had struggled with life's challenges and losses, as is true of any marriage. Now, only a handful of days together remained. Mel's health rapidly declined. Soon he was slipping in and out of consciousness. Eleanor patiently and lovingly cared for her husband and prepared to mourn.

The insurance company informed Eleanor that although Mel was going to die soon, it might not be soon enough for insurance to cover all the expenses. She needed to move Mel to hospice. So on a Friday in the summer of 1998, between visits to her dying husband, Eleanor set out with her daughters to find an insurance-approved hospice where her husband of fifty-seven years could spend his final days.

The next day, I made an early pastoral visit to the hospital. It was Saturday, so I didn't spend much time on my appearance. I wet my hair down so it wasn't sticking straight up, which was only partially effective. I skipped the shaving thing altogether. Like I said, it was early, and it was Saturday.

Things were grim at the hospital — monitors blinking and beeping, tangled IVs, and tubes. Mel, a big man who loved to hunt and fish, was breathing raggedly, slipping in and out of consciousness, dying in a room that smelled like medicine and worse.

I knew Eleanor was making hospice arrangements, so I didn't expect to see her early on a Saturday morning. Yet I had only been with Mel a few minutes when she breezed into the room. She smiled and said, "Hi, pastor," even as she went straight to Mel's side. She said to Mel, "Hi, honey," and gave him a kiss. As far as I could tell, Mel was unaware of her presence.

In contrast to her scruffy-looking young pastor, Eleanor could have been on her way to church or walking in from Christmas shopping. Her hair was nicely styled; she had applied makeup. I vividly remember she was wearing pretty red earrings that matched her lipstick. Feeling very underdressed, I went over to give her a hug and said, "Eleanor you look so nice. I like your earrings."

She leaned up and confessed with a whisper, "Pastor, I have to be honest with you. I'm so tired, I didn't know if I would have the coordination to put my earrings on in the morning. I put them on before I went to bed last night."

Mel died on Monday.

It is not a Hollywood script, but it is a beautiful story. Years later, both Mel and Eleanor are now with the Lord. I still picture

Eleanor putting in earrings before she went to bed to make sure she looked pretty when she went to see her dying, unconscious husband. It is a wonderful thing for a bride to be sure she looks beautiful walking down the aisle on her wedding day. But it is even more spectacular when, fifty-seven years later, the bride makes sure she looks pretty to walk down a hospital corridor to give her husband a final kiss good-bye.

What motivates such love, such loyalty, such courage in the face of death — such tender care? Some try to tell us that Eleanor's love for her husband is the result of billions of years of evolution. But I find the suggestion that her acts were nothing but a survival instinct ludicrous and insulting. Such an explanation cannot account for the beauty of marriage.

If you are amazed by the beauty of marriage, you are not alone. The authors of Scripture stood in awe of marriage too. In Proverbs 30:18 – 20, Agur confesses that the wonder of marriage is more than he can comprehend:

> Three things are too wonderful for me;
> four I do not understand:
> the way of an eagle in the sky,
> the way of a serpent on a rock,
> the way of a ship on the high seas,
> and the way of a man with a virgin.

Agur reflected on delicate images of God's glory in creation — an eagle floating in the air, a snake slipping across the rocks, a ship sliding across the waves. These pictures are beautiful in their own right, but they are on Agur's mind because he is thinking about marriage. When a man and woman come together in holy matrimony, the beauty is more than he can comprehend.[1]

Agur compares the beauty of marriage to that of a soaring eagle, but in the next verses he also contrasts the beauty of marriage to the revolting scenes of sexual immorality and an unloved woman:

> This is the way of an adulteress:
>   she eats and wipes her mouth
>   and says, "I have done no wrong."
> Under three things the earth trembles;
>   under four it cannot bear up:
> a slave when he becomes king,
>   and a fool when he is filled with food;
> an unloved woman when she gets a husband,
>   and a maidservant when she displaces her mistress.
>   Proverbs 30:20 – 23

By contrasting the beauty of marriage to the ugliness of immorality, Agur shows that he understood more than most. Still, he concedes that marriage is too wonderful for him to get his mind around.

While it may sound a bit presumptuous to say we could assist one of the inspired authors of Proverbs, we need to help Agur consider the beauty of stories like Mel and Eleanor's. The reason we can help Agur is that the New Testament gives insights into marriage that the other authors of the Old Testament could only long to glimpse (see 1 Peter 1:10). The apostle Paul explained in Ephesians 5:22 – 23 that there is a correspondence between Christ's relationship with the church and the relationship between husband and wife. Notice the words I've italicized:

> Wives, submit to your own husbands, as to the Lord. *For the husband is the head of the wife even as Christ is the head of the church, his body, and is himself its Savior.* Now as the church submits to Christ, so also wives should submit in everything to their husbands.
>
> Husbands, love your wives, as Christ loved the church and gave himself up for her, that he might sanctify her, having cleansed her by the washing of water with the word, so that he might present the church to himself in splendor, without spot or wrinkle or any such thing, that she might be holy and without blemish. In the same way husbands should love their wives

as their own bodies. He who loves his wife loves himself. *For no one ever hated his own flesh, but nourishes and cherishes it, just as Christ does the church*, because we are members of his body. "Therefore a man shall leave his father and mother and hold fast to his wife, and the two shall become one flesh." This mystery is profound, and I am saying that it refers to Christ and the church. However, let each one of you love his wife as himself, and let the wife see that she respects her husband.

Ephesians 5:22 – 33

Paul's point is that the gospel of Jesus and marriage explain one another.[2] A husband and wife are bound together in corporate solidarity, even as Christ is bound together with his body, the church. It follows, then, that to the extent that this book has helped you grow in your understanding of corporate solidarity, then you should be in a position to more deeply meditate on the wonder of marriage.

Keeping marriage in mind, let's review our progress in understanding corporate solidarity.

1. We have seen that understanding corporate solidarity is foundational to understanding the doctrine of original sin. When Adam sinned, he represented all of us. We are all guilty of sin. We are all corrupt. That is the bad news. The good news is the doctrine of union with Christ. If we believe in Christ, then we are united to him.

2. Corporate solidarity is also basic to the doctrine of the church (ecclesiology). We are not united with Christ as individuals. Rather, we are a part of his people, members of the body together, living in relationships with the rest of the body of Christ. Indeed, chapter 6 in this book emphasizes that we will never know the fullness of joy apart from sharing life with other believers.

Now here is an important point to remember as we seek to understand marriage more deeply. Given that the relationship between Christ and the church explains the marriage bond, the images Scripture uses to help us consider the bond between Christ and his church can help us understand the marriage union as well. Work through the pictures in your mind. A husband is united to a wife as bricks are to a building and as a head is to the body. Indeed, we even observe a correspondence between the marriage relationship and the intra-Trinitarian fellowship of the Father, the Son, and the Holy Spirit. This is not to say that the union of husband and wife is equivalent to the Trinity; rather, there is a correspondence between the two.

When we begin to see how intimately a husband and wife become one flesh, we appreciate the beauty of marriage even more. And we understand why it is so difficult for someone to lose a spouse. When I began pastoring the church I now serve, I introduced myself to an elderly man as he left church one Sunday. I said, "Hi, I'm Pastor Chris." He looked grimly back at me and said in a fierce voice, "I lost my wife." That was his introduction. It is what he thought I needed to know. I asked him his name, and he said, "Harold" — but as I greeted him that day, he wanted me to know his identity as a man who had lost his wife. He was torn in half. If Harold's leg had been amputated or his arm severed, those realities would have been obvious to me. He knew that the loss of his wife was not immediately apparent. So he told me, "I am a groom who has lost his bride."

I have heard people complain about a person deeply grieving the loss of a spouse. "They weren't even that close as a couple," someone says. A statement like that fails to understand what union of marriage means. Though the couple may have bickered daily, they were still one flesh. The surviving spouse still lost part of himself or herself. We really can't be too sensitive to those who lose their mate.

Understanding how a husband and wife are bound together helps us begin to make sense of difficult passages in Scripture. In Daniel 6, not only were the men who opposed Daniel thrown into the lions' den, but their wives and children were as well. Families are roped together. While this doesn't necessarily lead us to become comfortable with such judgment, it does show us how husbands and wives are viewed as one in the biblical world. When we avoid passages like this because we can't understand how wives suffer along with their husbands, we betray the fact that we do not understand the oneness of marriage.

Meditating on the corporate solidarity between husband and wife also helps us put divorce in the right perspective. Divorce is amputation. Amputation is only a last resort. When my cousin Tim was six years old, he was trying to play a trick on someone who was mowing the lawn. He ran up from behind, but his foot slid under the mowing deck. His leg was shredded. Physically speaking, Tim's accident was a nightmare from the beginning. The surgeon spent hours simply trying to find both ends of the main artery. Tim endured countless surgeries, went to school in a wheelchair, and endures chronic pain decades later. He tells me that as he lies in bed at night, his leg often just throbs.

Over the last fifty years, Tim has repeatedly faced questions: Should I let them amputate my leg? When is it no longer worth it to keep my knee and lower leg? These are difficult questions. Even though his leg will never be the same on this side of the resurrection, his leg is still a part of his body. So far he has kept the leg.

Tim lives with pain and walks with a limp, but he is whole.

Every marriage has painful moments because of significant sins and weaknesses in each spouse. When the pain becomes intense, divorce will be considered. We must realize that two have become one. If a divorce does take place, it will be like an amputation. Divorce is nothing short of severing a limb.

I'm not saying that divorce should never be considered any more than I'm saying a limb should never be amputated. If someone has gangrene in his or her foot, it has to be amputated. One spouse may be so infected with sin that divorce is necessary, but it must only be done as a last resort.[3]

Strengthening the Bond of Marriage

Just as there is great pain for people when the bond of marriage is broken, either through death or divorce, there can also be great joy and strength when the bond is strong. So how do you strengthen the bond of marriage? How does a married couple grow in their love for one another, developing a love that reflects and illuminates the love of the gospel, the love between Christ and his church? As we've seen, Paul in Ephesians 5 draws the analogy between marriage and our union with Christ. In this same passage he gives specific insight into how the complementary roles of husband and wife mirror this union.

The Biblical Role of Wives

Paul begins with wives: "Wives, submit to your own husbands, as to the Lord. *For the husband is the head of the wife even as Christ is the head of the church, his body, and is himself its Savior.* Now as the church submits to Christ, so also wives should submit in everything to their husbands" (Ephesians 5:22 – 24, emphasis added).

Paul says that wives are to *submit* to their husbands. In contemporary culture, I find any time the word *submission* is mentioned, it causes the hairs on the back of the neck to stand up. Most biblical imperatives can be shared from the pulpit, and people will nod affirmingly, even when they know it will be challenging to pursue. If I say, for instance, "love one another," no one disagrees, even though there are a lot of people in their world who are hard to love. If I say, "serve," people nod solemnly. They know Jesus set an example of servant leadership for us to follow. I often tell our congregation, "The fear of the LORD is the beginning of wisdom" (Proverbs 9:10), and when I speak of reverently trembling before God, our flock receives this very well. Yet when the concept of submission is raised, whether it has to do with employees submitting in the workplace, people submitting to church leaders, or wives submitting to husbands, you can almost feel the temperature rising in the room.

In the case of encouraging wives to submit to their husbands in marriage, hypothetical questions fill our minds. What if a husband tells his wife to rob Fort Knox? Doesn't saying that wives should submit to their husbands imply a lack of equality for women? To answer such objections, let's consider four reasons raising the subject of submission rubs us the wrong way today.

1. We tend to misunderstand what the word means in the context of the Scriptures. In the Bible, when wives are called to submit to their husbands, there is no suggestion that wives are in any way inferior or of lesser value and worth than their husbands. Scripture clearly teaches that both husband and wife are created equally in the image of God:

> So God created man in his own image,
>   in the image of God he created him;
>   male and female he created them.

> Genesis 1:27

We should also remember that our creation in the image of God — as male and female — is a reflection of the relationship of the perfect image of God the Son to his Father. The Son submits to the Father yet is equal in essence, sharing in the glory. His submission does not make him inferior in any way.

Biblical submission means we *voluntarily* yield to one another in love.[4] Wives are under no compulsion to submit to their husbands other than as an act of obedience to the Lord. They are to love their husbands by submitting, "as to the Lord." Hence, wives should think proactively and creatively about how they can help their home succeed in every way. As Tim and Kathy Keller write, "A wife is never to be merely compliant but is to use her resources to empower."[5]

2. Husbands are not perfect. I know you are shocked to read this. I can picture the response of those wives who share my appreciation for sarcasm. I hear them say with mock surprise, "You're kidding me. Our husbands are not perfect?" On behalf of husbands everywhere, I readily confess, "We are not perfect." To be sure, the reality of some husbands' imperfections make it very difficult for wives to lovingly support them. Some men are so low in their behavior that their wives have to do the figurative limbo to support them. Yet God knew husbands would not be perfect when he encouraged wives to be under their headship. The imperfections of their husbands do not excuse wives from fulfilling their biblical roles.

When speaking of submission in any context, it must be stated that submission or obedience to other human beings is *always* limited.[6] Scripture is clear that we ought to obey God rather than human beings (Acts 5:29). If a husband tried to lead in ways that require their family to sin, wives should not submit to their headship. For instance, Scripture does *not* expect women to submit to abusive husbands. Nor does God expect, answering the hypothetical question raised earlier, that wives would rob Fort Knox or do something illegal because a husband demanded them to.

While it is important to note that submission is always limited, I've observed that instances of husbands asking their wives to do something morally wrong are relatively rare. More often, when husbands are making a marriage difficult, it is because they have ongoing patterns of sin that drain the wife, though the husband is not requiring his wife to sin. For women in that situation, the first passage I recommend is 1 Peter 3:1 – 6, where Peter encourages women to win their husbands through inner beauty and godliness, through the "imperishable beauty of a gentle and quiet spirit, which in God's sight is very precious" (1 Peter 3:4).

3. Submission flies in the face of what our contemporary culture teaches. In 1998, the Southern Baptist Convention approved a statement on marriage and the family. Though I am not a Southern Baptist, I believe this statement is a concise, balanced, and well-written summary of biblical teaching. Read an excerpt for yourself:

> Marriage is the uniting of one man and one woman in covenant commitment for a lifetime. It is God's unique gift to reveal the union between Christ and His church and to provide for the man and the woman in marriage the framework for intimate companionship, the channel of sexual expression according to biblical standards, and the means for procreation of the human race.
>
> The husband and wife are of equal worth before God, since both are created in God's image. The marriage relationship models the way God relates to His people. A husband is to love his wife as Christ loved the church. He has the God-given responsibility to provide for, to protect, and to lead his family. A wife is to submit herself graciously to the servant leadership of her husband even as the church willingly submits to the headship of Christ. She, being in the image of God as is her husband and thus equal to him, has the God-given responsibility to respect her husband and to serve as his helper in managing the household and nurturing the next generation.[7]

The backlash to this statement was fierce. Marty Lasley, a Southern Baptist messenger from Tennessee, wrote an article with the title "Keeping Women in Servitude Down on the Plantation." Here is his introduction:

> It happened on June 10, 1998, at the annual meeting of the Southern Baptist Convention in Salt Lake City, Utah. While

the Oak Ridge Boys crooned a Southern Gospel version of The Rolling Stones' "Under My Thumb," several thousand white Southern Baptist pastors and their precious, meek, graciously submissive Stepford wives enthusiastically voted to turn back the clock to those antebellum "glory days" when white men ruled supremely over their women, children, servants and slaves because their Bibles told them so … The SBC ceremoniously reiterated its longstanding, Southern, patriarchal, chauvinistic view of man.[8]

Lasley's introduction is a perfect example of how authors ridicule the other party when their own position has little merit. He compares a biblical view of marriage roles to slavery, chauvinism, and the antebellum South. I'm not sure why he failed to compare Southern Baptists to Nazis. Yet, give him credit. He packed a great deal of sarcasm into a very small space. The only thing missing is a substantive argument as to why the Baptist position does not responsibly reflect the truth of Scripture. The Southern Baptist statement is very careful to say that men and women are of equal value. Their relationship corresponds to the relationship between God the Father and God the Son.

In our day, a steady stream of people says that submission in marriage is comparable to slavery. Too many of us have allowed this thinking to shape the way we see marriage. All believers must be sure that our minds are not conformed to the pattern of this world. Rather, we need to be transformed by Scripture so we can discern what is best and not be held captive by foolish arguments.

4. We *do* understand what submission means, and we don't like it. I remember the time our oldest daughter, Allison, was three, and I "required" her to do something, and she submitted … eventually. It had been quite a showdown between father and daughter. Afterward, as Allison sat on my lap, she tearfully said, "I just wish I was the queen of the whole world, and everyone had to do what I wanted them to do."

I told several family members about Allison's frustration. We all agreed we knew exactly how Allison felt. Rebellion is nothing new. The oldest temptation began with Satan telling Eve she would be like God if she ate the fruit. Adam and Eve wanted to do what they wanted to do. They did not submit, and our suffering is predicated on their rebellion. Like Adam and Eve, we are tempted to rebel rather than submit, but we must not give in to that temptation.[9] Rather, we must listen to the quiet promptings of the Holy Spirit and trust God to give us the strength to submit.

The Biblical Role of Husbands

For their part, husbands are called to love their wives in the same way Christ loved the church. Men have the tremendous privilege of leading their families, not through following their selfish ambitions, but through following Christ. Servant leadership is at the heart of how husbands are called to love their wives. Jesus illustrated servant leadership when he washed the disciples' feet (John 13:1 – 17). It does not require a doctorate in the culture of the ancient Near East to know that foot washing was a servant's job. Because this custom is no longer observed in the modern world, we husbands need to think creatively about the mundane "servant" jobs we should take the lead in doing in our homes. Scripture is clear that we husbands should be looking for opportunities to clean the bathrooms, wash the dishes, take out the trash, fold the laundry, or carry out whatever other humble task is required at home. If you have an infant still in diapers, it's quite clear where you can look for opportunities for servant leadership.

One of the most important ways a husband can serve his wife is by taking leadership in saying, "I'm sorry. Will you please forgive me?" No Christian husband would ever claim perfection in marriage. But sometimes a husband believes his wife was *more* wrong, and he expects his wife to be the first to say, "I'm sorry." But this isn't servant leadership. The husband who is committed to humble servant leadership will lead the way in asking for forgiveness, especially when it's hard to be the first to say, "I'm sorry."

Another way husbands can love their wives in a Christlike manner is by being good listeners. I confess that too many times I'm a lousy listener. Sometimes when my wife, Jamie, is bringing me up to speed on a current issue in our family, I'm impatient and say something stupid like, "Cut to the chase." I thank God I have a gracious wife. But she and I are bound together, and it is sin when I as a servant leader do not listen to her.

Of course, the ultimate example of servant leadership did not take place when Jesus washed the disciples' feet. The core of how Christ showed his love for the church is that he died on the cross. We husbands must always remember that we are called to love our wives in a cross-centered way. If a sacrifice needs to be made for the sake of the family, a husband and father should be first in line.

Philip Bliss was a famous musician and a key member of D. L. Moody's ministry team in Chicago. Bliss and his wife were returning to Chicago on a bitterly cold day in the winter of 1876. Kerosene was being used to heat the passenger cars, and as the train crossed a bridge near Ashtabula, Ohio, a trestle gave way and the railcars plunged to the bottom. The train immediately caught fire, but Bliss managed to crawl out of the wreckage. Yet once he had escaped the wreck, he immediately realized that his wife was still trapped inside. Without hesitating, he went back to rescue her. In the end, both of them perished in the fire.

Bliss understood. Husbands are called to love their wives *sacrificially*. Though this example vividly illustrates a husband's willingness to lay down his life for the sake of his wife, the biblical challenge does not just refer to a one-time event. This sacrificial love should characterize a husband's actions every day in the decisions and choices he makes. In some ways, daily sacrificial love is more difficult than a one-time sacrifice. Giving your life in love for your wife over the long haul means being patient with her, caring for her as you would care for your own body. Learning to love like this is not a sprint, filled with occasional bursts of gracious love; it is a marathon marked by a consistent pattern of putting the needs and desires of your family under the guidance of God.

●   ●   ●

Throughout this book, I have acknowledged that it is extremely difficult for people in our culture to understand the idea that we are bound together in corporate solidarity. We should see that to the extent it is difficult for us to understand how individuals are bound together, it is also difficult to have a biblical vision for marriage. So we must meditate on this truth. Husband and wife are one flesh. The relationship between a husband and wife is as strong as a hand to a wrist. They are one flesh. They are bound together.

CHAPTER EIGHT

A Red Rope for Hurting Families

Happy families are all alike; every unhappy family is unhappy in its own way.

Leo Tolstoy, *Anna Karenina*

Madrid is full of boys named Paco, which is the diminutive of the name Francisco, and there is a Madrid joke about a father who came to Madrid and inserted an advertisement in the personal columns of *El Liberal* which said: PACO MEET ME AT HOTEL MONTANA NOON TUESDAY ALL IS FORGIVEN PAPA, and how a squadron of Guardia Civil had to be called out to disperse the eight hundred young men who answered the advertisement.

Ernest Hemingway, "The Capital of the World"

A wise son makes a glad father, but a foolish son is a sorrow to his mother.

Proverbs 10:1

"O my son Absalom, my son, my son Absalom! Would I had died instead of you, O Absalom, my son, my son!"

2 Samuel 18:33

How do you comfort someone who has a family member making poor decisions? For my nearly twenty years as a pastor, I have been prayerfully considering how to answer that question. What does a pastor say to a mother or father whose adult son is homeless because of drug addiction? Or to parents whose children have been arrested for a felony? Or to those whose children have denied the faith? What do you say to the father of a prodigal who has despised his family and traveled to a far country to squander his inheritance in riotous living (Luke 15:13)?

How does a pastor comfort a man who found his unrepentant wife in bed with another man? How do you counsel a wife whose husband tells her she must accept his infidelity as a way of life?

If you are going through the pain of a wayward child, an unfaithful spouse, or some other broken family relationship, my heart goes out to you. I'm not sure there is any category of pain worse than family pain. I've watched people battle cancer, heart disease, and paralysis. I've seen others lose jobs and careers. Yet, in my own experience and in my observation as a pastor, the pain that comes from having a rebellious family member is uniquely devastating.

Even if you haven't endured the pain of a loved one turning away from Christ, you have undoubtedly seen the varied emotions of those whose family members have let them down. Some are angry. Husbands blame wives, and wives blame husbands. Some point an accusing finger at the youth group or church in which they or their children never connected. Some beat themselves up, convinced they have failed those they love the most. Others toss and turn in bed, wondering where their son or daughter or husband or wife will spend eternity.

Many who have family members making decisions with eternally negative consequences simply live in denial. They don't even ask for prayer. They refuse to face the reality that their loved one will spend eternity apart from Christ. Who among us can dwell on that possibility for people we love? Yet that possibility is there.

I approach this chapter humbly. I haven't arrived at a definitive solution on how to minister to those who have family pain. Complete resolution to that problem awaits Christ's return. But the principle of the rope becomes deeply practical in this area of ministry. If you are in pain over a loved one, I pray you will find some comfort here.

First, the principle of the rope helps us understand why rebellion and discord in our family result in such deep hurt. We are not isolated individuals. Our family members are a part of us, and we are a part of them. When one of our family members makes poor choices, we feel the pain of the consequences as though a limb was infected or even severed. This is the picture C. John Miller used in his highly recommended book titled *Come Back, Barbara* as he describes how he felt when their daughter turned her back on her family and her faith: "I was stunned, brokenhearted, and ashamed. I sensed something that I never felt from Barbara before ... the whole subtle message that she was ashamed of us and our Christianity ... [My wife] and I felt we were experiencing an amputation, a violent cutting away of part of our flesh. And the severing had not been a clean one — though it certainly was complete."[1]

Miller's description of an amputation is consistent with the idea of solidarity or the principle of the rope. When Barbara distanced herself from her family, part of them was torn away, ripped from their family body. The pain felt by people for family members is very real.

Second, the principle of the rope also shows how we can respond to and process rebellion in our family. As I focus on this topic for the rest of the chapter, I am primarily concerned to encourage those with rebellious family members to remember this: *the rope to Christ and the gospel is exceedingly stronger than the rope to Adam and sin.* The good news is good more than the bad news is bad. If we keep in mind that the rope of the gospel is stronger than the rope of sin, we have the beginnings of a rescue strategy for rebellious family members.

Yet, far more biblical reflection is needed than to simply say that the gospel rope is stronger. I will begin with a curious choice of Scripture texts — the battle of Jericho. This may seem to be the most unlikely place in Scripture to look for comfort for hurting family members. After all, God's command to destroy the Canaanites is one of the Bible's most difficult teachings. But as I've stressed throughout this book, rather than avoiding those passages that bring tension, we should meditate on them, knowing that we may be feeling tension because these passages point to areas where our thinking needs to be shaped by Scripture. If you are hurting because of decisions made by members of your family, I think you will find comfort and encouragement in this chapter.

Devote All of Jericho to Destruction

The battle of Jericho was the first major step in Israel's conquest of the Promised Land. Israel's mission regarding the Canaanites who inhabited the land was clear. God had expressly commanded Israel to destroy them:

> "When the LORD your God brings you into the land that you are entering to take possession of it, and clears away many nations before you, the Hittites, the Girgashites, the

Amorites, the Canaanites, the Perizzites, the Hivites, and the Jebusites, seven nations more numerous and mightier than you, and when the LORD your God gives them over to you, and you defeat them, then you must devote them to complete destruction. You shall make no covenant with them and show no mercy to them."

Deuteronomy 7:1 – 2

Within Canaan, Jericho was the first city Israel encountered after crossing the Jordan River. God gave specific instructions for that battle:

The LORD said to Joshua, "See, I have given Jericho into your hand, with its king and mighty men of valor. You shall march around the city, all the men of war going around the city once. Thus shall you do for six days. Seven priests shall bear seven trumpets of rams' horns before the ark. On the seventh day you shall march around the city seven times, and the priests shall blow the trumpets. And when they make a long blast with the ram's horn, when you hear the sound of the trumpet, then all the people shall shout with a great shout, and the wall of the city will fall down flat, and the people shall go up, everyone straight before him." So Joshua the son of Nun called the priests and said to them, "Take up the ark of the covenant and let seven priests bear seven trumpets of rams' horns before the ark of the LORD."

Joshua 6:2 – 6

While these instructions outline an unusual battle strategy, the theological point is clear. With the promise that the walls of Jericho would be supernaturally demolished, God was establishing that Israel would prevail only because he was with them. The Israelites would not win the battle because they had devised an ingenious plan or had been particularly valiant. It was God who would win the victory.

While local churches are not called to wage military campaigns like Israel was, we still have an applicable truth to consider.

As much as the Israelites needed the help of God if they were to defeat Jericho, we must also rely on Christ. We can only be truly victorious if the hand of the Lord is with us. Proverbs 21:31 reads, "The horse is made ready for the day of battle, but the victory belongs to the LORD." We can and should prepare. Yet we will only prevail with God's help. Likewise, when it comes to family struggles, we need God's help, and this should move us to fervent prayer. Before you say, "Oh, I pray all the time," I would press back. "Do you really pray? Are you getting together with other Christians and getting down on your knees and crying out to God? Have you fasted and prayed? Are you journaling your prayers?"

Joshua and Israel obeyed the Lord and followed the battle plan. They marched silently around Jericho for six consecutive days. If someone tried this today, "silently" wouldn't work because surely someone's cell phone would ring. Yet Israel silently circled Jericho. It must have been ominous for all involved. Outside Jericho was the dust of marching, shuffling of feet, rattling of armor, and the long, solemn processional. Inside the walls of Jericho was the smell of fear. Leaders shouted instructions. Soldiers slept at their posts. Rumors rippled throughout the city. All of Jericho looked out at the strange processional marching around their walls and prepared to fight to the death.

On the seventh day, with the ark of the covenant before them, the Israelites marched around Jericho seven times. When Jericho saw that Israel was going to march around more than one time, they must have been aware that this day was different and that the battle was imminent. With each successive lap, the tension built. Israel was silent, but surely from within Jericho insults were being hurled.

After the seventh time that Israel marched around the city, the trumpet was blown. As soon as they heard the blast of the trumpet, the Israelites "shouted a great shout" (Joshua 6:20), and God immediately flattened the walls of Jericho.

It must have been utter chaos. Dust filled the air. People screamed in pain. Haughty soldiers who had been perched high on the walls shattered limbs as they fell into the rubble. Some probably fell on the sharp edges of their own weapons. The entire defense system for Jericho was destroyed. Into this chaos, Israel's army charged, and Scripture tells us, "They devoted all in the city to destruction, both men and women, young and old, oxen, sheep, and donkeys, with the edge of the sword" (Joshua 6:21).

Everyone in Jericho died — men, women, children, and livestock. Can you picture the scene? What did it look like for children to be executed? What did the air of Jericho smell like? What kind of sounds would you hear? It's a scene none of us care to imagine, except that it is recorded in Scripture and written down as a warning for us (1 Corinthians 10:11). The destruction of Jericho was a time of astonishing judgment.

Yet one family was spared. Rahab — the prostitute who had hidden Israel's spies when they were doing reconnaissance on Jericho. She and her family were allowed to live (Joshua 6:17).

The complete destruction of Jericho raises the thorny question of why God ordered Israel to kill everyone in Jericho. We'll take up that question soon. But before we do, let's focus on the gospel in the life of Rahab. Her story contains great encouragement for those with struggling family members.

The Gospel in the Life of Rahab

Rahab and her family were spared destruction because she had hidden the Israelites who were doing espionage in Jericho (Joshua 2:1 – 4). It is hard to imagine the risk that hiding Israel's spies posed for Rahab. Jericho was a cruel and evil place. If Jericho's leaders had discovered that Rahab was harboring the enemy, she and her family would most certainly have been tortured and murdered.

Scripture records Rahab's explanation of why she hid the spies:

> Before the men lay down, [Rahab] came up to them on the roof and said to the men, "I know that the LORD has given you the land, and that the fear of you has fallen upon us, and that all the inhabitants of the land melt away before you. For we have heard how the LORD dried up the water of the Red Sea before you when you came out of Egypt, and what you did to the two kings of the Amorites who were beyond the Jordan, to Sihon and Og, whom you devoted to destruction. And as soon as we heard it, our hearts melted, and there was no spirit left in any man because of you, for the LORD your God, he is God in the heavens above and on the earth beneath. Now then, please swear to me by the LORD that, as I have dealt kindly with you, you also will deal kindly with my father's house, and give me a sure sign that you will save alive my father and mother, my brothers and sisters, and all who belong to them, and deliver our lives from death."
>
> Joshua 2:8 – 13

Rahab had decided to put her faith in the God of Israel rather than in the idols of Jericho.

Rahab's story reminds me of a book I read when I was growing up — *The Hiding Place*, the true story of Corrie ten Boom and her family who hid Jews during World War II in their home in the Netherlands. The ten Boom family understood that if the Nazis discovered the Jews, it could well mean their own death. It is a story of amazing courage. Rahab's actions were just as incredible as the ten Boom family's resistance against the Third Reich, perhaps even more so. Rahab defied the "Nazi" leaders of Jericho, knowing that being caught would mean something worse than being gassed in a concentration camp.

While Rahab's actions were courageous, she isn't the one we should be amazed by in the story of the fall of Jericho. After all, Scripture tells us she was a prostitute. The most amazing character in the story is God, whose grace pardons Rahab, even though she deserved death. If anyone is tempted to accuse the God of the Old Testament of not being merciful and gracious, they need to read the Joshua account again. Even though Rahab was a sinful woman in an evil city, God was merciful and gracious to her. She trusted God, and he gave her the gift of grace.

God's grace wasn't limited to Rahab. Because of Rahab's courage, Israel's spies promised that her entire family would be spared. Her agreement with the spies included her family.

> Then she let them down by a rope through the window, for her house was built into the city wall, so that she lived in the wall. And she said to them, "Go into the hills, or the pursuers will encounter you, and hide there three days until the pursuers have returned. Then afterward you may go your way." The men said to her, "We will be guiltless with respect to this oath of yours that you have made us swear. Behold, when we come into the land, you shall tie this scarlet cord in the window through which you let us down, *and you shall gather into your house your father and mother, your brothers, and all your father's household.* Then if anyone goes out of the doors of your house into the street, his blood shall be on his own head, and we shall be guiltless. But if a hand is laid on anyone who is with you in the house, his blood shall be on our head. But if you tell this business of ours, then we shall be guiltless with respect to your oath that you have made us swear." And she said, "According to your words, so be it." Then she sent them away, and they departed. And she tied the scarlet cord in the window.
>
> Joshua 2:15 – 21, emphasis added

By virtue of letting the spies down with a rope, and with a red rope in her window, Rahab indicated that she and her family were trusting in the God of Israel rather than in the idols of Jericho. Rahab and her family were bound together with Israel rather than Jericho. When Rahab made the decision to fear the Lord, not only was she saved; her family was saved as well.

Now I quickly add that Rahab's family was *not* saved by virtue of Rahab's faith. Each of them also had to make the decision to trust in the God of Israel. Any one of them could have burst out of their home and betrayed Rahab to the leaders in Jericho. Yet, if it hadn't been for Rahab's courage, no one else in her family would have possessed the fortitude to risk everything by hiding the spies.

If one of your family members is making poor decisions, remember that the principle of the rope is more powerful in the gospel than in condemnation in Adam. According to Romans 5:12 – 21, what Christ did is parallel on one level to what Adam did — but *far* more powerful. If evil people are dragging down your family members, be encouraged: Christ is more powerful than the sin that is dragging down your children or spouse!

To be sure, the principle of the rope in Jericho was very real in a negative direction. The entire city of Jericho had rebelled against God and was under God's judgment. All were to die. They were all roped together — children and livestock included. Yet for Rahab, who believed, the rope of the gospel was far greater than the rope of sin.

Neither the judgment poured out on Jericho nor the grace given to Rahab should surprise us, considering what God had told Moses decades earlier:

> The LORD passed before him and proclaimed, "The LORD, the LORD, a God merciful and gracious, slow to anger, and abounding in steadfast love and faithfulness, keeping steadfast love for thousands, forgiving iniquity and transgression and sin, but who will by no means clear the guilty, visiting the iniquity of the fathers on the children and the children's children, to the third and the fourth generation."
>
> Exodus 34:6 – 7

The passage stresses that the principle of solidarity is true in both directions. When the fathers rebel against God, there are consequences to the third and fourth generation. Thankfully, the power of the gospel is far greater than the power of sin. For those who follow Christ, tens of thousands are affected.

For those who feel great pain for their families, I commend to you the story of Jericho and Rahab. Even when it looks as though things can't possibly work out, don't underestimate the power of God's grace. Hide the spies. Take a chance for Christ. Put a red rope in the window of your home. Identify with the Lord Jesus Christ. Perhaps God will be pleased to save not only you but your mother and father and your sisters and brothers as well.

Spend less time going over and over in your mind the decisions your family members have made, and spend more time growing in grace. I know a mother of adult children who is deeply concerned about the choices her children are making. She responds by renewing her efforts to attend prayer meetings and to pray for her family. I know another mother, who in her concern about her college-age son, stayed up late to write out a long prayer for him. God only knows how he will use faithful mothers who choose to be on their knees for their family members.

Yet, if you turn to bitterness rather than prayer, if you give in to the temptation to pout and try to manipulate the situation, then the consequences can be devastating for your entire family.

You may respond, "I've already made so many mistakes in life. What I've done has way too many negative consequences for my family. It's too late." To that I would counter, "Read the first six chapters of Joshua again." Do you not remember what Rahab did for a living? She was a whore. The Bible repeatedly reminds us of Rahab's history. Nearly every time Rahab comes up in Scripture, she is called "Rahab the prostitute." Even in the New Testament, when her example is favorably cited in Hebrews 11:31 and James 2:25, she is identified as "Rahab the prostitute." If I were her, I would have wished the Scriptures would drop the harlot label and call her "Rahab of Jericho." Her lifestyle is included so we never forget that the story is all about the grace of God, who is quick to forgive those who turn and put their trust in him.

Do not buy the lie that it is too late for your family. Do not buy the lie that your sins are too great. Run to the cross. Hang a red cord out your window. Put your trust in Jesus, and the grace of God will abound to you and your family.

Others of you will object, "I *have* put my faith in Christ. I *have* followed him for decades. In spite of that, my parents, my sons and daughters — or even my spouse — keep turning their backs on Christ. Things only seem to be getting worse."

Be patient. The last chapter is not yet written. You cannot imagine how God, who works all things together for good for those who have been called according to his purpose, will bring the story together. Be still and know that God is God. Wait for Christ.

> Have you not known? Have you not heard?
> The LORD is the everlasting God,
>   the Creator of the ends of the earth.
> He does not faint or grow weary;
>   his understanding is unsearchable.
> He gives power to the faint,
>   and to him who has no might he increases strength.
> Even youths shall faint and be weary,
>   and young men shall fall exhausted;
> but they who wait for the LORD shall renew their strength;
>   they shall mount up with wings like eagles;
> they shall run and not be weary;
>   they shall walk and not faint.
>
> Isaiah 40:28 – 31

This is not to imply that the idea of biblical solidarity is some sort of ironclad guarantee that if only you follow Christ, all your family will do so as well. Scripture makes no such promise. No one can guarantee that if you do the right thing, your family members will all repent and turn to Christ. Indeed, the point of chapter 5 in this book is that *each of us is responsible* for choosing to follow Christ.

Yet if you personally walk with Christ, you cannot begin to imagine how God will work in and through your life. If you choose to follow him, you will affect your family in ways that are beyond all you can ask or imagine. The fruit of your faithfulness may not be seen until long after you are dead and gone; indeed, you will *not* see all the fruit of your faithfulness in this life. But be assured: you can store up treasure in heaven where moth and rust cannot destroy and where thieves cannot break in and steal (Matthew 6:19 – 21). Follow Christ. He will graciously put a lever on your life and use you in amazing ways for all of eternity.

The story of Rahab only gets better after the book of Joshua. Rahab shows up again in the Gospels. Matthew begins his gospel with the genealogy of Jesus. At first glance, the genealogy seems like only a list of names. Those who use reading plans to read through the Bible often wonder if they need to actually read each name to say they have read the Bible. Here's my advice: do read them closely. For those who know Old Testament background, these genealogies contain strong clues about the grace of God.

The first thing that catches our attention in this list is the inclusion of women. One would not expect women to have been included. And if women *were* included in the genealogy of Christ, then the first three choices would have been the obvious ones: Sarah, Rebekah, and Rachel, the beautiful matriarchs of Israel. But the four women included in this genealogy are Tamar, Rahab, Ruth, and Bathsheba.

Space does not permit me to review their stories in detail. Suffice it to say that humanly speaking, these four women would have been the last four anyone would have chosen to be included in the genealogy. They were all Gentiles who had scandalous pasts. Tamar had pretended to be a prostitute in order to seduce her father-in-law, Judah (see Genesis 38). Whereas Tamar only pretended to be a prostitute, Rahab actually was one. Ruth was a Moabitess, a descendant of Lot's drunken, incestuous relationship with his daughter (see Genesis 19:30 – 38). Bathsheba and David were guilty of the most infamous case of adultery in history (see 2 Samuel 11).

Why does Matthew include in this list four Gentile women with scandalous backgrounds? The obvious answer is that the good news of Christ is a story that is all about grace. The point of the unfolding plan of salvation is not that God uses a group of people who had it all together. Quite the opposite — their lives were messy. Yet for those who turned and put their faith in Christ, God was so gracious as to use them within his plan of salvation.

I think back to Rahab, with a red rope hanging out of her window, while Israel's army prepared to attack. I picture her terrified family huddled together in a dark home, assuming they might well be murdered by either the people in Jericho or the army of Israel. Children wailing. Men and women softly crying. Some trying to be brave.

The pastor in me wishes I could have been there. I would have whispered in Rahab's ear, "It's going to be OK. God has something for you and your family that is beyond anything you can ask or imagine. Not only will you be spared, but your family will too. And one day you will be a part of the lineage of the one true King."

I don't have that opportunity with Rahab. She doesn't need a pastoral whisper from me. She lived and died by faith. She is now in the presence of the King. But I *can* whisper to those reading this book. I know things may look impossible. But listen, based on the gospel of the Lord Jesus Christ, let me assure you that you cannot picture how the situation will turn around for you or for your family. Look to Christ. Trust in him. God will work in and through you in ways that are beyond all you can ask or imagine

(Ephesians 3:20 – 21). How God will use you will unfold across generations to come, even as it did with Rahab. You can count on it.

Why Did God Order Israel to Kill Everyone in Jericho?

Lest you think I'm trying to evade the tough questions, we now need to consider why God ordered the complete obliteration of the Canaanites, including the inhabitants of Jericho. We can understand on some level that the evil leaders and the army of Jericho had to be put to death. But kill *everyone* and *everything*? Livestock? Toddlers? Babies? It seems too awful to even consider.

Over the years, a number of different explanations have been offered for God's order that the Canaanites be destroyed. Those who do not hold a high view of Scripture have suggested that the God of the Old Testament is different from the God of the New Testament. Not only does this reveal a low view of Scripture; one wonders as well if these people have even read the book of Revelation. The judgment described in Revelation is every bit as graphic as the judgment pictured in the Old Testament. In fact, Jesus himself warned about the coming judgment of God, often using vivid language to describe the agony of those judged by God.

Others suggest that God did not actually order Israel to destroy the Canaanites but that Israel destroyed the Canaanites of their own accord. Again, such an interpretation would require that Scripture errs when it explicitly states that *God commanded Israel* to "destroy them totally" and "show them no mercy" (Deuteronomy 7:2). Of course some, in one way or another, even deny the historicity of the account — a view that directly contradicts God's Word.

We can make a few additional points to help us understand the severe judgment of the Canaanites. First, the Canaanites had been given a great deal of time to repent. Rahab acknowledged that Jericho was well aware of the judgment of God (Joshua 2:10 – 11). Like Nineveh during the time of Jonah, they could have repented (Jonah 3:10). God is gracious and merciful, slow to anger and abounding in steadfast love (Jonah 4:2). Yet only Rahab and her family chose to turn from their wickedness. It is not as though they weren't given an opportunity for repentance. Just as people had ample time in the days of Noah, so they had a chance to repent before Israel's conquest of the Promised Land.

The fact is that the Canaanites were a terribly wicked people. A number of passages (for example, Leviticus 18; 20:22 – 24; Deuteronomy 9:5; 12:29 – 31) make it clear that the Canaanites were characterized by gross sexual sin and even child sacrifice. When the whole catalog of decadence in Canaan is reviewed, we see it truly was an awful place. Christopher Wright summarizes, "Now if we take all these texts seriously as part of God's explanation for the events that unfold in the book of Joshua, we cannot avoid their implications. The conquest was not human genocide. It was divine judgment."[2]

The destruction of Jericho should serve as a sobering warning about the justice and holiness of God. It is only a preview of God's final judgment. Those who refuse to believe in Christ — the one who absorbed the wrath of God on behalf of his people — will face a Jericho judgment soon enough (see 1 Corinthians 10:11 – 12). As the apostle John writes, "Whoever believes in the Son has eternal life; whoever does not obey the Son shall not see life, but the wrath of God remains on him" (John 3:36).

Finally, in the destruction of Jericho we see that solidarity is real. In God's created world, people are not seen as atomistic individuals. We are bound together. Jericho families died together. Tremper Longman III speaks to this point: "We must point out that the Bible does not understand the destruction of the men, women, and children of these cities as a slaughter of innocents.

Not even the children are considered innocent. They are all part of an inherently wicked culture that, if allowed to live, would morally and theologically pollute the people of Israel."[3]

I am not saying this is an easy conclusion to accept. Indeed, it is very difficult to swallow. Yet, even as I anticipate readers pushing back against the negative consequences of solidarity, we must also remember it is only through the reality of identification with Christ that we have hope. To insist that we should all be isolated individuals is to argue against the gospel. The only reason we can be saved is because the One can represent the many.

Encouragement for Those Hurting Because of a Family Member

If you are hurting because of the decisions your family members have made, my heart goes out to you. Your pain is real. We are not isolated individuals. We are roped to one another and to our family in particular ways. When one of our family members chooses to jump off a moral cliff, we suffer with him or her.

Yet even as you grieve, focus on the hope of the gospel. Remember that the principle of the rope is more powerful in the positive than in the negative. Christ's victory is greater than Adam's transgression. If you follow Jesus, rest in the hope that God will use you in your family's life in ways that you cannot even begin to imagine.

Think again of Rahab. She was a prostitute! Yet when she chose to put her faith in the God of Israel, God saved not only her but her family too. Surely she struggled with the baggage of being a prostitute for the rest of her life. No doubt she had many nightmares. Yet the power of the gospel continued to work, long after she died. Amazingly, she was included in the line of Jesus Christ, and the example of her faith is cited in Hebrews 11 alongside Abraham, Moses, and Noah: "By faith Rahab the prostitute did not perish with those who were disobedient, because she had given a friendly welcome to the spies" (Hebrews 11:31).

What positive steps can you take to grow as a man or woman of faith? Have you spent time fervently praying with other believers? Is there any area of sin where you continually compromise? Grow in grace. Hide the spies. Hang a red rope out your window. Look to the cross. It is not about us earning something for our families; rather, it is about trusting in Christ and what he did on the cross.

Even as you consider Rahab's positive example, heed the warnings of Scripture. Perhaps you are contemplating walking away from Christ. Maybe you are angry with God and blame him for your family member's sin. Maybe you're already living in rebellion to God. Somehow you have bought the lie that judgment will not be too bad, that what you do is strictly your own private affair, and that you have the right to be angry. It is a lie that we can mock God without suffering any consequences (see Galatians 6:7). God's judgment is real. He is a consuming fire. Our response can only be to kneel at the cross and worship him with reverence and awe (see Hebrews 12:28 – 29). It is a lie that what we do is strictly our own affair. We are roped to our families. We dare not take a path that will cause a bitter root to grow up in our lives, thereby defiling many. Let us lift our feeble arms and strengthen our weak knees and run with perseverance the race marked out for us (see Hebrews 12:1 – 3, 12 – 17). Think "we," not "I." As Solomon states, "In the fear of the Lord one has strong confidence, and his children will have a refuge" (Proverbs 14:26).

All Christians Have a Family

We must remember that the fundamental family identity for any Christian is our adoption into a new family, a new tribe. We are part of a new story with a new identity. Just as Rahab was adopted into Israel when she renounced Jericho, we also are a part of God's unfolding story of redemption.

Perhaps some of you have lost family members because of the trust you have placed in Christ. But this does not mean you are orphans. Russell Moore encourages:

> We know the first Christians were persecuted. What we don't think about often is how lonely many of them must have been. Many of them would have been told by their parents, their siblings, their spouses, and their villages not to speak to them again until they pulled themselves out of the fisherman's cult. The Spirit of adoption didn't just wrench them away from their family ties. He gave them new ones. The Messiah they followed told them that those who leave behind "houses or brothers or sisters or father or mother or children or lands, for my name's sake, will receive a hundred-fold and will inherit eternal life" (Matthew 19:29). Through adoption into Christ, the word *brother* means something.[4]

To be united with Christ means to be bound together with him in a new family. This does not mean our hearts don't hurt deeply for those we love, but it does mean we have a new identity in our Savior.

CHAPTER NINE

A Rescue Rope for Those Facing the Fear of Death

"We've all got to go through enough to kill us."
Burley Coulter, in Wendell Berry, *A Place on Earth*

It's not that I'm afraid to die, I just don't want to be there when it happens.
Woody Allen, *Without Feathers*

Death presents society with a formidable problem not only because of its obvious threat to the continuity of human relationships, but because it threatens the basic assumptions of order on which society rests ... The power of religion depends, in the last resort, upon the credibility of the banners it puts in the hands of men as they stand before death, or more accurately, as they walk inevitably towards it.
Peter Berger, *The Sacred Canopy*

As by a man came death, by a man has come also the resurrection of the dead. For as in Adam all die, so also in Christ shall all be made alive.
1 Corinthians 15:21–22

I recently watched the movie *Valkyrie*, a World War II story about a group of German officers who attempted to assassinate Adolf Hitler. Even if you have not seen the movie, you probably remember from history class that the plot failed and the officers were executed by a firing squad. The final scene was powerful — men standing before their executioners without a blindfold, looking down the barrel of death, knowing the end was only a few seconds away. I wondered how I would respond in such a situation? Could Jesus *really* help me face death without terror? How about you? Is Jesus really close enough to help us today?

As you consider how you might respond if you faced imminent death, think of our apparent distance from Christ. The death, burial, and resurrection of Jesus Christ are remote in every scientific dimension. Geographically, Jesus lived on the other side of the world, a place few of us will ever visit. Temporally, Jesus was crucified nearly two thousand years ago. The American Revolution, or even Christopher Columbus's voyage, compared to the time of Jesus was recent. Culturally, Jesus grew up in a working-class Jewish family. He didn't own an iPad or check Facebook after a long day of teaching and healing. Chances are quite good there wasn't even a Wi-Fi connection at the Starbucks in Nazareth. Amazing!

Can Jesus really help us have courage in the face of death? Consider the question *critically*. Why should believing in Jesus have anything to do with being able to face death without fear? If you are a Christian, you will rightly respond, "Jesus died on the cross so we could be delivered from the penalty for our sins and become a part of his people and his kingdom." That is absolutely true. As Paul wrote concisely in Romans 8:1, "There is therefore now no condemnation for those who are in Christ Jesus." Yet the question remains: How is it that what Jesus did helps *us* face death? How is it possible that someone so far away could help us *now*?

The question of how Jesus helps his people face death without fear is one the recipients of the letter to the Hebrews were pondering. While the original audience of Hebrews was not nearly so far removed from Jesus as we are in the twenty-first century, Jesus still seemed a great distance away.

Confidence in the Face of Death from Hebrews 2:10 – 18

Long before the time of the Nazis, first-century Christians in and around Rome faced a situation comparable to Jews during the Holocaust. They lived under the thumb of the wicked and insane Roman emperor Nero, who was every bit as "certifiable" as the evil lunatic Adolf Hitler.

Nero started at a young age. His mother, the vile Agrippina, successfully schemed and murdered so that Nero was installed as emperor at the age of seventeen. Agrippina's plan was to serve as coregent with her son. In the beginning, Nero played along, allowing Seneca and others to lead. The empire ran smoothly. Soon, however, Agrippina thirsted for more power, and as she began scheming, Rome became "a devil's brew of murder and intrigue."[1]

Nero had his mother murdered in AD 59. Apparently, he did not feel particularly indebted to her for scheming to put him in power. From then on, it was clear that Nero was a lunatic who would have made a villain from *Batman* look sensible. His insanity is evidenced in his response to the great fire in Rome in July 64. Nero had been away when the fire began. He returned and was rumored to admiringly watch the flames while playing a lyre.

Rumors soon circulated that Nero not only admired the flames but also had started the fire because he wanted to build in the area where the blaze initially began. Imagine the outrage when people heard that their leader was entertained by the catastrophe and was rumored to have ordered it.

Nero needed a scapegoat. He decided to blame the Christians. Persecution and difficulties quickly multiplied. Believers faced the possibility of imminent death.[2] It was to these believers that the book of Hebrews was written.

We don't know who wrote the letter to the Hebrews. We do know the author enjoyed a close relationship with his readers. He knew his recipients had faced persecution but things had been better for a time (10:32). Now they were again facing the possibility of brutal persecution and were tempted to renounce their faith. Indeed, some were already beginning to drift away and were sporadic in their church attendance (2:1; 10:25). Others were tempted to return to Judaism.[3]

In the face of such a grim situation, the author of Hebrews encouraged his audience by assuring them that they need not fear death because in Christ they have a victorious champion. The idea of Christ as our victorious champion is found in verse 10 of chapter 2, where the author describes Christ as the "founder" of our salvation: "For it was fitting that he, for whom and by whom all things exist, in bringing many sons to glory, should make the founder of their salvation perfect through suffering."

The word translated "founder" carries both the ideas of leader and champion, as well as founder.[4] For those familiar with the Old Testament, it carried the idea of God's people being led, most notably by Moses when he led the Israelites out of Egypt. The author of Hebrews reminds his readers that they have a champion who is even greater than Moses.[5]

For someone from a Jewish background, the fact that Christ is a greater champion than Moses would have been compelling. Yet, there was a challenge in encouraging Christians by referring to Moses. Moses had physically been in Egypt. Christ was not physically present in Rome. He was not bodily in their midst. Was Christ really one of them? The author of Hebrews knew it would not be enough to merely say that Christ is a victorious champion. These Christians needed something more than a remote historical figure who is unrelated to their suffering in Rome. They needed the certainty that Christ is in solidarity with his people.

To use the terms of this book, the author of Hebrews understood that if Christians were to be confident in the face of death, they must first be confident *they are truly bound to Christ*. This point of Christ's solidarity with his people is being established in Hebrews 2:10 – 18. Notice the phrases in bold that emphasize Christ's union with his own:

> For it was fitting that he, for whom and by whom all things exist, in bringing many sons to glory, should make the founder of their salvation perfect through suffering. For he who sanctifies and those who are sanctified **all have one origin**. That is why he is not ashamed to call them brothers, saying,
>
> > "I will tell of your name **to my brothers**;
> > in the midst of the congregation I will sing your praise."
>
> And again,
>
> > "I will put my trust in him."
>
> And again,
>
> > "Behold, I and the children God has given me."
>
> **Since therefore the children share in flesh and blood, he himself likewise partook of the same things**, that through

death he might destroy the one who has the power of death, that is, the devil, and deliver all those who through fear of death were subject to lifelong slavery. For surely it is not angels that he helps, but he helps the offspring of Abraham. **Therefore he had to be made like his brothers in every respect**, so that he might become a merciful and faithful high priest in the service of God, to make propitiation for the sins of the people. For because he himself has suffered when tempted, he is able to help those who are being tempted.

Hebrews 2:10 – 18

Meditate on the emphasis on solidarity. Hebrews 2:11 tells us that Christ who sanctifies and those who are sanctified all have one source. This sentence might be literally translated, "Both the one sanctifying and those being sanctified are all of one." Here is another strong reference to union with Christ. Those who know Christ are *one* with him who sanctifies and sets them free. Believers are bound together with Jesus. Unbelievable! For the Christian, there is nothing remote about Jesus because we are united with him.

Hebrews 2:12 – 13 quotes both Psalm 22 and Isaiah 8. Each stresses that Christ is family with his people. The reference to Psalm 22 is wonderful to consider. You will recall that Psalm 22 is the prophetic psalm of the Lord's passion quoted by Jesus on the cross, "My God, my God, why have you forsaken me?"[6] Quotations or allusions to Psalm 22 are woven into each of the four gospel accounts.[7] While the first part of Psalm 22 deals with Christ's death on the cross, a transition is made at verse 22, and the vindication of Christ is anticipated: "I will tell of your name to my brothers; in the midst of the congregation I will praise you" (Psalm 22:22). The author of Hebrews quotes this verse to assure his readers they have solidarity with Christ. He is encouraging them to remember that they are part of the fulfillment of what was promised. Christ considers them brothers. He is in their midst through the power of the Holy Spirit.[8]

Psalm 22:22 – 31 describes four characteristics of the "great congregation" (Psalm 22:25) with whom Jesus will have solidarity.

1. Christ has solidarity with "you who fear the LORD" (Psalm 22:23), i.e., with believers. Christ is one with those who reverently bow their knee to the King and give their lives to him. Remember what the apostle John wrote: "To all who did receive him, who believed in his name, he gave the right to become children of God" (John 1:12). Amazing!

2. Christ has solidarity with the afflicted. Psalm 22 emphasizes that Christ hears the cries of the brokenhearted.

> For he has not despised or abhorred
>   the affliction of the afflicted,
> and he has not hidden his face from him,
>   but has heard, when he cried to him.
> From you comes my praise in the great congregation;
>   my vows I will perform before those who fear him.
> The afflicted shall eat and be satisfied;
>   those who seek him shall praise the LORD!
> May your hearts live forever!
>
> Psalm 22:24 – 26

Perhaps you feel as though you could never be worthy of being included in the people of God. Of course, you are right. *None* of us could ever be worthy of Christ. Yet, Christ is worthy. He paid the penalty for sin. He did so for those who know they have nothing to offer — for the broken and afflicted.

3. Christ has corporate solidarity with a great congregation from throughout the earth. The gospel goes out, as we read in Psalm 22:27, to "all the ends of the earth." Indeed, the Great Commission declares that we are to go into all nations and make disciples (Matthew 28:18 – 20). No island is too remote for the Lord Jesus Christ. He brings justice to the nations (Isaiah 42:1).

4. Christ is the corporate head of people who come from across all ages: "They shall come and proclaim his righteousness to a people yet unborn, that he has done it" (Psalm 22:31). We

need not fear that the gospel is historically remote. It has always been God's plan that his people would come from across the centuries. Until Christ returns, he will continue to gather his people from across the ages.

The Incarnation

In Hebrews 2:14 the author of Hebrews points to the incarnation as the theological basis for Christ's solidarity with his people. Since we have flesh and blood, he shared our humanity in order that he might be roped to us. We need to pause for a moment and carefully consider the doctrine of the incarnation. John Murray stated that "the incarnation means that he who never began to be in his specific identity as God, began to be what he eternally was not."[9] With precision, the Westminster Confession of Faith states, "Two whole, perfect, and distinct natures, the Godhead and the manhood, were inseparably joined together in one person, without conversion, composition, or confusion."[10]

Notice the qualification given in the last part of this sentence: no conversion — God was not changed; no composition — a third hybrid was not formed that involved both deity and humanity; no confusion — deity and humanity are not a mixture. God became flesh and blood so he might have solidarity with his people and win the victory on their behalf. Christ was roped together with us so he could win the victory on our behalf.

Robert Letham compares the incarnation to the idea of a teammate acting on behalf of the entire team.

> [Christ's] work is ours because we are on the same team. If, in a game of soccer, the goalkeeper makes a massive blunder and lets in the decisive goal at the last minute, the whole team loses the game. Conversely, if the striker, with seconds left, scores a brilliant goal to win the game 3-2, the whole team participates in the victory. In a similar way, Christ has made atonement and won the victory for his team.[11]

We need not imagine ourselves in Nazi Germany or ancient Rome to grasp the importance of this text. The legitimacy of Christ's solidarity with his people is no less important for us today. Soon enough, you and I will face death. It may be instantly in a car accident; it may be after a prolonged battle with cancer. Whatever the case, if Jesus of Nazareth is to have any significance for us as death approaches, it can only be because we are truly united to him. Hebrews 2:10 – 18 establishes beyond question that the solidarity of the believer with Christ allows him or her to go through life without being a slave to the fear of death.

Four Ways Christians Benefit from Their Solidarity with Christ

The author of Hebrews does more than merely establish the fact of the believer's solidarity with Christ. In this rich section, he identifies four ways that Christians benefit from their solidarity with Christ.[12]

1. Christ established solidarity with believers so he could bring many sons and daughters to glory (2:10). How do you picture glory in your mind? I tend to think of sports images. The United States defeated the Soviet hockey team at Lake Placid in the 1980 Olympic Games. As the game came to an end, the announcer Al Michaels shouted into the microphone, "Do you believe in miracles?" It was a glorious victory, the most exciting American sports victory of my lifetime. However, compared to the glory believers will share in Christ, it is not even worth talking about. It was child's play, a backyard pickup game. Christ is bringing many sons and daughters to *glory*. Those who know him can look forward to the most spectacular celebration in history. Therefore, as the apostle Paul stated, "we do not lose heart ... For our light and momentary troubles are achieving for us an eternal glory that far outweighs them all" (2 Corinthians 4:16 – 17 NIV).

2. Christ established solidarity with believers so he could "deliver all those who through fear of death were subject to lifelong slavery" (2:15). History bears witness to the truth that believers do face death without fear. Indeed, John Calvin viewed the testimony of Christian martyrs as firm proof for the credibility of Scripture:

> Now with what assurance ought we to enlist under that doctrine which we see confirmed and attested by the blood of so many holy men! They, having once received it, did not hesitate, courageously and intrepidly, and even with great eagerness, to suffer death for it. Should we not accept with sure and unshaken conviction what has been handed on to us with such a pledge? It is no moderate approbation of Scripture that it has been sealed by the blood of so many witnesses, especially when we reflect that they died to render testimony to the faith; not with fanatic excess ... but with a firm and constant, yet sober, zeal toward God.[13]

I think of the number of times as a pastor I have witnessed Christians resting peacefully in Christ in their final hours. I have never seen a growing believer who has despaired in the face of death. I have seen other people despair — in fact, one inconsolable man haunts my memory. Yet I have not seen mature believers give way to fear.

3. Christ established solidarity with believers so he "might become a merciful and faithful high priest in the service of God, to make propitiation for the sins of the people" (2:17). A priest stands between one party and God. Gerry Breshears writes, "He is an intermediary, representing another person in the presence of God and bringing the presence of God to the person."[14] Christ became one of us so he might make intercession with the Father. Because we have Christ as our great high priest, we can rush confidently into the presence of the Father to find help in our time of need (Hebrews 4:16). Further, Christ made propitiation for our sins. He absorbed in his body the punishment we deserved so we would no longer be objects of wrath.

4. Christ established solidarity with believers so he could "destroy the one who has the power of death, that is, the devil" (2:14). Satan is very real, despite what the voice of contemporary culture may say. One would think our culture would learn something from the last one hundred years. It is tragically ironic that German theologians in the early twentieth century denied that Satan existed, only to have the Third Reich personify the reality of the Evil One. Frederick Dale Bruner observed, "A progressive national theology in Germany dismissed the demonic as myth and then experienced the hyper-demonic forces of Nazism with Nazism's own perverse demonology of the devilish Jew."[15] Satan is real. Scripture tells us he prowls around like a roaring lion (1 Peter 5:8). He would like nothing more than to destroy your life. He will succeed if you are not united with Christ. However, if you are bound to Christ, you can be sure that Christ will soon destroy him.

The Story of Count Helmuth James von Moltke

Thirty-seven-year-old Count Helmuth James von Moltke was sentenced to be hung by the Nazis on January 23, 1945. Moltke was aware that the Nazis' preferred method of execution was to hang the victim naked with piano wire. He went to bed in his jail cell with the certain knowledge he would soon die.

Political execution was a most unlikely ending for Moltke. From childhood, he was expected to be a great leader in Germany. He had been born into an aristocratic family. His great-uncle was a war hero. And when that uncle died childless, Moltke became the heir of a title and a beautiful estate.

Moltke, however, did not coast on the reputation of his family. He studied international law in Breslau, Berlin, and Vienna.

He was prepared for a life of influence in Hitler's Germany. Yet Moltke detected early that Nazism was evil. He declined appointment as a judge because it would have required him to join the Nazi party. Instead, he accepted an appointment in London.

When the war broke out, Moltke began working secretly to oppose the Third Reich. Eventually, he was arrested for speaking critically of Hitler. Yet, even in a Nazi prison cell, Moltke's faith continued to grow as his suffering increased. He and other Christians encouraged one another with the Word. When they had no opportunity to speak personally, they would whistle the tune of a Christian hymn when they passed in the prison yard.

Students of history will know that in January 1945 when Moltke was sentenced to death, the Allied forces were only months away from V-E Day — victory in Europe. It would be too late for Moltke. With confidence in his Savior, he wrote a letter to his wife:

> My dear heart, first, I must say quite obviously the last twenty-four hours of my life are in no way different from any others. I always imagined that one would feel shock, that one would say to oneself: Now the sun sets for the last time, now the clock only goes to twelve twice more, now you go to bed for the last time. None of that is the case. I wonder if I am a bit high, for I can't deny that my mood is positively elated. I only beg the Lord in heaven that he will keep me in it, for it is surely easier for the flesh to die like that. How merciful the Lord has been to me! Even at the risk of sounding hysterical: I am so full of gratitude that there is hardly room for anything else. He guided me so firmly and clearly these two days ... It was truly as it says in Isaiah 43:2: when thou passest through the waters, I will be with thee; when thou walkest through the fire thou shall not be burned; neither shall the flame kindle upon thee.[16]

Moltke was certain God had been providentially ordering every step of his way to be prepared to die for Christ. He wrote these words:

> For what a mighty task your husband was chosen: all the
> trouble that God took with him, the infinite detours, the
> intricate zigzag curves, all suddenly find their explanation
> in one hour on the 10th January 1945. Everything acquires
> its meaning in retrospect, which was hidden … It has all
> become comprehensible in a single hour. For this one hour
> the Lord took all that trouble.[17]

Moltke faced death with confidence because he knew he was bound together with Christ.

Few of us will face death in circumstances so historically charged as the murder of Moltke. I doubt any counts will read this book. The Third Reich has long since been defeated. Nevertheless, if Christ does not return, we will all face death soon. Death hurts. It is ugly. It stings. But we need not fear it. Our champion, the second Adam, the Lord Jesus Christ, has won the victory. He took on flesh and blood so he might establish solidarity with us. He won the victory at every turn. Now, as our great High King he makes intercession on our behalf.

I have seen people terrorized by the fear of death. I was once invited to talk with a man who was in the last hours of his life. He was fully conscious, very alert, but every breath was an effort. There was no time for "friendship evangelism," no chance he would even visit our church. I gently said to him, "Well, it looks as though you will soon stand before God." He replied, somewhat flippantly, "Well, I won't be the first." He refused to even consider what he faced. I read to him the account of the criminals crucified alongside Jesus (Luke 23:39 – 43). I asked him to consider the difference between the man who railed at Jesus and the one to whom Jesus said, "Truly, I say to you, today you will be with me in Paradise." Sadly, he wasn't interested in talking about eternity. Looking back on it, I wonder if he was scared.

I have known others who were visibly scared. I think of one man who lay on his deathbed crying, wishing he had lived his life differently. This need not be so. If you know Christ, you can rest in him. He took on human flesh to establish solidarity with us and to free us from our fear of death.

Know that the rope between Christ and his people is firm; it will not break. We can fall from the highest cliff, yet we need not fear. The rope that binds us to Christ is the unchanging reality of his incarnation and the good news of his atoning death on our behalf. Because Christ has solidarity with us in his life and in his death, we are guaranteed that we will also share in his resurrection and in the promised inheritance of eternal life with him.

For more on how you can be sure of your salvation, see "The Gospel and Assurance of Salvation" on pages 187 – 192.

CHAPTER TEN

Roped Together in Country and Culture

The early settlers bequeathed to their descendants the customs, manners, and opinions that contribute most to the success of a republic. When I reflect upon the consequences of this primary fact, I think I see the destiny of America embodied in the first Puritan who landed on those shores, just as the whole human race was represented by the first man.

Alexis de Tocqueville, *Democracy in America*

The marvelous new militancy which has engulfed the Negro community must not lead us to a distrust of all white people, for many of our white brothers, as evidenced by their presence here today, have come to realize that their destiny is tied up with our destiny. And they have come to realize that their freedom is inextricably bound to our freedom. We cannot walk alone.

Martin Luther King Jr., "I Have a Dream"

Religion legitimates social institutions by bestowing upon them an ultimately valid ontological status, that is, by locating them within a sacred and cosmic frame of reference.

Peter Berger, *The Sacred Canopy*

I pray that the sharing of your faith may become effective for the full knowledge of every good thing that is in us for the sake of Christ.

Philemon 6

I began this book by noting that the idea of solidarity seems strange to the late modern mind. I conclude by stating that if we love the places and people where and with whom we live, we need to befriend this strange idea of solidarity, and do so very quickly. A biblical view of corporate solidarity is essential, not only for churches and families, but also for countries and cultures. Recovering a biblical view of solidarity is foundational to moving forward into a prosperous future. If we Westerners continue to see ourselves as islands, the future will be very dark. Cultures and countries cannot flourish apart from a deep recognition of solidarity that only Christ and his church can make happen.

Stated more technically, here is the point of this chapter: (I warn you that I have borrowed language from sociologists, and so it is a bit of a mouthful.) *Only New Testament churches can offer the plausibility structures needed to legitimatize solidarity and counter the radical individualism unraveling the fabric of Western culture.*

Such a statement immediately raises a number of questions:

- What is radical individualism, and how does it threaten Western culture? Is individualism *always* bad?
- What are "plausibility structures," and is there any biblical warrant for believing they are important?
- How are local churches uniquely qualified to counter radical individualism?
- Specifically, what must churches do to counter this radical individualism?

These questions provide a framework for this chapter. However, before going any further, I should say a word about why I extensively interact with sociologists in this chapter. I am not suggesting that sociology provides *authoritative* answers for the problems we face. Only God's Word has final authority and wisdom to address these challenges. Be assured that before this chapter concludes, we will turn to Scripture. However, like the tribe of Issachar in the Old Testament, we need to learn to wisely apply God's Word to our current cultural situation.[1] Sociologists offer great help in this "Issacharian" endeavor of understanding our times.[2] Indeed, we can be thankful for brilliant minds that understand the situation of late modernity and have issued such prescient warnings.

The Rise of American Solidarity

We begin with one such warning from a young French political theorist more than 180 years ago. In 1831, twenty-six-year-old Alexis de Tocqueville set sail to tour a country that was itself only fifty-four years old. Tocqueville's official reason for visiting was to evaluate the penitentiary system. Unofficially, he wanted a firsthand opportunity to assess why the democratic experiment in the United States had been so uniquely successful after failing in other contexts. Tocqueville believed there were important lessons to be learned from the United States that would benefit his own country of France. While Tocqueville spent less than two years in the United States, it is now clear that his assessment was brilliant. He understood why America had succeeded and identified a threat to which he believed the United States would be uniquely susceptible.

Tocqueville's overall evaluation of the country was positive. He marveled, "Where in the memory of man can one find anything comparable to what is taking place before our eyes in North

America?"[3] As to reasons for America's success, Tocqueville posited that a unique combination of factors had coalesced to produce a nearly ideal country. He organized these factors into three categories.

1. Tocqueville believed that God's providence had blessed America with *an abundance of natural resources*. He marveled, "Everything about the Americans is extraordinary, their social state no less than their laws. But what is still more extraordinary is the land on which they live ... There one sees, as in the first days of creation, rivers that never run dry, verdant, well-watered solitudes, and boundless fields yet to be tilled by any plow."[4]

2. Tocqueville believed that America's greatness was partially due to *the specific form of government* the people had developed. The American experiment in government combined the strength and power of a great republic with the security of a smaller one. Local governments counterbalanced the federal government, and the judicial system provided an effective check against the excesses of the majority.[5]

3. Most relevant to our discussion, Tocqueville believed that a common culture of Christian morality had created *a virtuous society*. He himself did not embrace traditional Christian doctrine, but he believed that the religious foundation of Christianity had immensely benefited America.[6] He wrote, "There is no better illustration of the usefulness and naturalness of religion, since the country where its influence is greatest today is also the country that is freest and most enlightened."[7] Tocqueville explained that in the United States, Christianity reigned "without impediment, by universal consent."[8] His point was not to suggest that the specific *form* or structure of government was Christian or biblical.[9] Further, Tocqueville insisted it was *not* his goal in his evaluation of democracy in America to advocate an intrusive form of government.[10] Indeed, "Tocqueville marveled at the relative absence of government from American life and the corresponding vitality

of civil society, especially when compared to the state's all-pervasive presence in his native France."[11] Tocqueville believed it was Christian values and virtues, what he called "habits of the heart," rather than the involvement of government that made for responsible citizens.[12] This, he suggested, was the bedrock of the American experiment.

Tocqueville was not naive about the spirituality of America. He understood that not every citizen was a professing Christian. He was aware of the fact that even among those who professed faith in Christ there was still great hypocrisy. Even so, he noted, "Revolutionaries in America are obliged to profess a certain public respect for Christian morality and equity, so that it is not easy for them to violate the laws when those laws stand in the way of their own designs. And even if they could overcome their own scruples, they would still be held in check by the scruples of their supporters."[13]

Tocqueville was especially impressed by the effectiveness of American homes in passing along Christian "habits of the heart," and the strength of American homes began with a high regard for marriage: "Of all the countries in the world, America is surely the one in which the marriage bond is most respected, and in which people subscribe to the loftiest and most just ideal of conjugal happiness."[14]

Tocqueville believed that mothers, in particular, deserved high praise for teaching Christian values to their children. Positioning himself to be quoted in Mother's Day sermons for centuries to come, Tocqueville wrote, "If someone were to ask me what I think is primarily responsible for the singular prosperity and growing power of [Americans], I would answer that it is the superiority of their women."[15]

Christian "habits of the heart," instilled by godly parents living together in committed marriages, had given rise to a citizenry with a strong sense of civic responsibility and solidarity with one another. George Washington, for example, exemplified the deep recognition of solidarity that compelled citizens to place the good of the country ahead of personal desires. Long before Washington retired, he had desired to withdraw from public service. Yet Washington said that when he reflected on the critical junctures at which the United States found itself, he was duty bound to serve. Even when Washington did retire, he said he could do so with a clear conscience only because he was sure it would not harm the country: "I beg you, at the same time, to do me the justice to be assured that this resolution has not been taken without a strict regard to all the considerations appertaining to the relation which binds a dutiful citizen to his country."[16] It was this commitment to the ties that bind a dutiful citizen to his country, exemplified in Washington but found in so many citizens, that Tocqueville argued was fundamental to America's success.

Tocqueville was careful to note that the United States was not a perfect country. Indeed, he envisioned an ominous scenario in which the trajectory of America would take a turn for the worse. To express his concerns for America, Tocqueville introduced a word he was among the first to use — *individualism*. He defined individualism as "a reflective and tranquil sentiment that disposes each citizen to cut himself off from the mass of his fellow men and withdraw into the circle of family and friends, so that having created a little society for his own use, he gladly leaves the larger society to take care of itself."[17] Tocqueville said the roots of this new individualism could be observed in that "Americans, who mix so easily in political assemblies and tribunals, are careful by contrast, to divide into very distinct small associations to savor the pleasures of private life apart from others. Each freely recognizes all his fellow citizens as his equals, yet he never receives more than a small number as his friends and guests."[18]

Tocqueville reasoned that an unhealthy emphasis on this new type of individuality might eventually lead to excesses in which people no longer saw themselves in solidarity with the rest of the country. If people began to see themselves as mere individuals who have lost the solidarity that bound them together, there would no longer be sufficient citizenry to serve the common good of the nation as a matter of principle and commitment. In the worst case, this would be the result:

> I see an innumerable host of men, all alike and equal, endlessly hastening after petty and vulgar pleasures with which they fill their souls. Each of them, withdrawn into himself, is virtually a stranger to the fate of all the others. For him, his children and personal friends comprise the entire human race. As for the remainder of his fellow citizens, he lives alongside them but does not see them. He touches them but does not feel them. He exists only in himself and for himself, and if he still has a family, he no longer has a country.[19]

In the event that the United States became radically individualized, Tocqueville warned that the government would be nothing better than a machine enabling a citizenry of petulant brats:

> Over these men stands an immense tutelary power, which assumes responsibility for securing their pleasure and watching over their fate. It is absolute, meticulous, regular, provident, and mild. It would resemble paternal authority if only its purpose were the same, namely, to prepare men for manhood. But on the contrary, it seeks only to keep them in childhood irrevocably. It likes citizens to rejoice, provided they think only of rejoicing. It works willingly for their happiness but wants to be the sole agent and only arbiter of that happiness. It provides for their security, foresees and takes care of their needs, facilitates their pleasures, manages their most important affairs, directs their industry, regulates their successions, and divides their inheritances.[20]

Just as parents who spoil their children also demean them and stunt their ability to truly mature, a government that spoils its citizens will debase them by removing from them all motivation to grow up and think for themselves. Tocqueville said this would be a kind of "soft despotism" that crept in almost unnoticed.[21] If a government begins to spoil its citizens in this way, Tocqueville wondered, "Why not relieve them entirely of the trouble of their thinking and the difficulty of living?"[22] After all, such a government discourages true growth: "Every day it thus makes man's use of his free will rarer and more futile. It circumscribes the action of the will more narrowly, and little by little robs each citizen of the use of his own faculties."[23]

Tocqueville believed radical individualism was a real threat to the future of the United States. Left unchecked, it will unravel the fabric of society and lead to a new strain of tyranny.

The Problem of Radical Individualism

Today many of the concerns articulated by Tocqueville have come to fruition. The individual is seen as ultimate. Consequently, we have witnessed a decline of civic virtue at the expense of the common good. In addition, the loss of an objective standard for determining what is good and healthy for society has left us with nothing but a vague cultural desire to respect diversity and tolerate the perspectives and choices of others. Radical individualism is undermining the corporate solidarity that gave rise to our national success.

To be clear, not all individualism is bad. As we saw in chapter 5, the decisions of individuals matter. There is room for legitimate expressions of our individualism, and Scripture is full of examples of individuals who made decisions that God used to accomplish his purposes for the good of his people. One need only read Hebrews 11 to be reminded of a long list of individuals who made momentous decisions. Not all individualism is to blame.[24] Instead, what we are talking about is *radical* individualism, the belief that individuals have no fundamental relationship or obligation to the rest of society. This denial of the principle of the rope is terribly destructive.

David Wells clarifies the difference between the radical individualism seen today and a healthy understanding of individualism that recognized accountability to higher principles and community obligations:

> Last century's individualism was one in which personal responsibility played a large role. It was the kind in which people thought for themselves, provided for themselves, owed nothing, and usually worked out their independence within a community ... This produced the kind of person who ... was "inner-directed." That is, this person was guided by an internal gyroscope of character and belief and, as a result, saw it as a virtue to have clear goals, to work hard, to live by ethical principle. This ... is the kind of person who would rather be right than be president.
>
> Today's individualist, by contrast, would rather be president than be right. It is not character that defines the way that expressive individualism functions today, but emancipation from values, from community, and from the past in order to be oneself, to seek one's own gain.[25]

Today the autonomous self ("self in a castle," according to Scot McKnight) is seen as ultimate. An individual's right to choose is considered sacred. Freedom is defined as "getting to do whatever I want, when I want, and how I want."[26] Describing a new generation of emerging adults who are radically individualistic, Christian Smith summarizes, "According to emerging adults, the absolute authority for every person's belief or actions is his or her own sovereign self. Anybody can literally think or do whatever he or she wants."[27] In another of his books, Smith observes, "American youth, like American adults, are nearly without exception profoundly individualistic, instinctively presuming autonomous, individual self-direction to be a universal human norm and life goal."[28]

One of the most thorough studies of the corrosive effect of radical individualism on American society is found in the book *Habits of the Heart*, first released in 1985. Taking the title from Tocqueville's phrase, Robert Bellah and a team of sociologists concluded that Americans were increasingly turning inward. They observed that the radical individualism present in American culture was effectively cutting its own throat by diminishing the very institutions and traditions that had first championed the rights of the individual: "The absolute commitment to individual dignity has ... seemed to invalidate the biblical and republican traditions. And in undermining those traditions, as Tocqueville warned, individualism also weakens the very meanings that give content and substance to the ideal of individual dignity."[29]

When the individual is ultimate, there is no legitimate reason for people to serve the countries and institutions that protect them as individuals. People will still be motivated to run for office and serve in government, but they are not truly looking to "serve." Radical individualism leads one to aspire to political office because it is viewed as an individual accomplishment. Christian Smith picks up on this in describing the lack of interest emerging generations have about politics: "Almost all emerging adults today are either apathetic, uninformed, distrustful, disempowered, or, at most marginally interested when it comes to politics and public life. Both that fact itself and the reasons for it speak poorly of the condition of our larger culture and society."[30]

Judge Robert Bork has also argued that radical individualism will unravel the foundations of our culture and, paradoxically, lead to the *loss* of individual rights. It will do so by attacking the role and authority of the family and the church. In other words, what first began in America as an attempt to protect the rights of the individual will ultimately destroy those very rights.[31]

Nowhere is the point that radical individualism leads to tyranny more clearly seen than in the instance in which a woman's "right to choose" licenses her to collaborate with doctors to end the life of her own baby. Only the most radical individualism could contend that a mother has the individual right to become a murderous tyrant over her own baby.

Why Radical Individualism Persists Today

Our age seems to have a hate-love relationship with radical individualism. On the one hand, one has to stand in a long line if he or she is to criticize the new strain of individualism. D. A. Carson has pointed out, "Not many voices are raised these days in support of individualism ... In short, on all sides we are being taught that individualism dominates Western thought, and it is bad."[32]

Yet even as we rail against individualism, we continue to love being isolated. As a pastor, I have observed that some of the people who say they miss the sense of community that was enjoyed forty years ago are often the most withdrawn from church fellowship. Brimming with nostalgia, they speak longingly of the times when small towns gathered on Saturday nights. Nevertheless, they refuse to attend church events, including the sacraments of baptism and Communion. And in their refusal to be a part of community, often because they use "family obligations" as the excuse, they are blind to the hypocritical tension between saying they long for community in one breath while refusing it with the next.[33]

Let me be clear. I do not think that people are consciously insincere when they say they want community but decline to participate. The majority actually do want to share life together. They recognize the dangers of individualism but are unable to do anything about it. Why is it so? To answer this question, it is helpful to flesh out a term coined by sociologist Peter Berger — "plausibility structures." Berger used this term to refer to the structures of community that reinforce and teach people the values that are necessary to hold a society together:

Beliefs become plausible if they are supported by the people around us. We are all social beings, we were created as social beings and much of what we think about the world depends on support by important people with whom we live. That's what I call plausibility structure, and religion is no exception to this. So it would be very difficult to be a Catholic in a Tibetan village. It would be difficult to be a Buddhist in a Catholic village in the south of Italy. That's what I mean by plausibility structure.[34]

James Davison Hunter, an American sociologist of religion and culture, echoes this same point and explains that beliefs are not easily changed because existing structures resist change:

"Worldview" is so deeply embedded in our consciousness, in the habits of our lives, and in our social practices that to question one's worldview is to question "reality" itself … This is why one cannot merely change worldviews or question one's own very easily. Most of what really counts, in terms of what shapes us and directs us, we are not aware of; it operates far below what most of us are capable of consciously grasping.[35]

The concept of plausibility structures helps us understand why we are so powerless to counter radical individualism, even when most people agree it is corrosive. For the past one hundred years, the values, messages, and worldview that have given rise to this radical exaltation of the individual, with the resulting negating of civic responsibility, have become deeply embedded into our modern consciousness. Today, people "are limited to a language of radical individual autonomy … They cannot think about themselves or others except as arbitrary centers of volition."[36] We no longer have a language in which to discuss or express the values, beliefs, and understandings that support the principle of the rope, our corporate solidarity with one another. This is confirmed by the observation repeatedly made in this book that the whole idea of our being bound together strikes modern sensibilities as very strange.

The question in countering radical individualism then becomes, "Where will we find structures to teach us that we are bound together?" According to Peter Berger, the answer is religion. It is religion that provides a "sacred canopy" so a society can function in a healthy way and maintain its solidarity in the face of chaos, particularly in the face of death. Only religion provides a structure that shows people they are deeply connected to one another. Berger writes, "Every human society is, in the last resort, men banded together in the face of death. The power of religion depends, in the last resort upon the credibility of the banners it puts in the hands of men as they stand before death, or more accurately, as they walk inevitably, towards it."[37]

To put all of this in simple terms, when we complain that we do not like our individualism, we are like fish saying we do not enjoy being wet. We swim in the waters of radical individualism, and it is not easy for us to "dry off," no matter how much we may see the need. The waters of radical individualism cannot simply be "wished" away — they must be replaced with something new and different.[38]

Why the Church Is Uniquely Qualified to Counter Radical Individualism

Thus far in this chapter three points have been established:

1. Radical individualism is unraveling the fabric of Western culture.
2. Identifying the threat is not enough to counter it because of the deeply embedded plausibility structures that perpetuate it.
3. A leading sociologist believes that only religion can offer the plausibility structures needed to counter radical individualism.

We are now in a position to appreciate the central argument of this chapter: it is not simply religion in general but Christianity in particular that can counter radical individualism. Indeed, *only New Testament churches can offer the plausibility structures needed to legitimatize solidarity and counter the radical individualism unraveling the fabric of Western culture.* Put another way, only New Testament churches can provide the community needed to counter radical individualism.

As I have said, a person in the West who wants to resist being radically individualistic is like a fish trying to think itself dry. Of course it will never happen. In the first place, fish cannot survive outside of water. If a fish is to undergo change, it must find a different pond in which to swim. Likewise, humans are social beings, and they will not survive outside of relationships. It is local churches that can provide "water" or plausibility structures that not only teach solidarity but also live it out in community with one another.

The necessity of an alternative community is why James Davison Hunter reasons that "there is a sociological truth, then, to the statement … 'there is no salvation outside the church.'"[39] He explains, "As a community and an institution, the church is a plausibility structure and the only one with the resources capable of offering an alternative formation to that offered by popular culture."[40] Obviously, this doesn't mean conversion can only take place in a formal church setting. Anyone who calls on the name of the Lord is saved. However, it does mean that people who will move beyond radical individualism will need to do so in the context of a local church.

The Biblical Emphasis on Community

At the beginning of this chapter, I promised that after considering the observations of sociologists, I would build an argument based on the authority of Scripture. To that end, let me point to an intriguing verse in the often neglected book of Philemon. In Paul's letter to Philemon, the apostle's goal is to motivate Philemon to be reconciled with Onesimus, who had been Philemon's slave before running away. In that sense, the letter is about a problem between two individuals. Yet the entire letter of Philemon demonstrates how the early church was anything but individualistic. Even though the primary focus is on an issue between two people, Paul addresses his correspondence to the entire church.

In the brief letter of Philemon (the entire book is only twenty-five verses long), Paul seeks to motivate Philemon on the basis of love — love for Christ, for Paul, and for the body of Christ. Though it is tempting to unpack the entire letter, let's focus on verse 6 and its role in Paul's argument for reconciliation: "I pray that the *sharing* of your faith may become effective for the full knowledge of every good thing that is in us for the sake of Christ" (Philemon 6, emphasis added).

Sharing is a translation of the Greek word *koinonia*, sometimes translated "fellowship" — a translation that is a bit unfortunate in our culture. It is often associated more with Super Bowl or World Cup parties and bean dip than with true community. However, in the first century, the word *koinonia* carried the idea of "invested partnership."[41] In encouraging Philemon to reconcile with Onesimus, Paul encourages him that he will not be able to fully understand all that we have in Christ if he approaches Christ on a purely individual level. Rather, Philemon must be active in Christian community if he is to appreciate the wonder of the gospel. If Philemon and Onesimus are not reconciled, then their experience of the Christian faith will be compromised.[42]

Paul next argues for the importance of community in a positive way. He assures Philemon that his joy has grown through being roped with Philemon: "I have derived much joy and comfort from your love, my brother, because the hearts of the saints have been refreshed through you" (Philemon 7). This is the point of chapter 6 in this book: *Christian joy will grow only to the extent that we grow in active fellowship with the body of Christ.*

Putting Philemon 6 and 7 together, a sociologist's paraphrase might read, "I pray that you will be a part of the plausibility structure of the church; if you don't, you will not be able to really understand your faith or what you should do. After all, Philemon, you have already refreshed me through your commitment to refreshing the hearts of the saints in Christian community." Paul knows Philemon will make the right decisions about Onesimus only if he does so in the context of solidarity with the Christian community.

Paul's strategy of addressing an interpersonal conflict within the larger context of the Christian community is evident throughout the entire letter. Notice how Paul begins the letter by bringing to the forefront the relationships in the fellowship: "Paul, a prisoner for Christ Jesus, and Timothy our *brother*, to Philemon our beloved *fellow worker* and Apphia *our sister* and Archippus *our fellow soldier*, and the church in your house" (Philemon 1 – 2, emphasis added).

In applying the timeless truth of Philemon to the current challenges of radical individualism, it should be clear that solutions must be pursued within the context of Christian community. Sound doctrine alone will not be enough to counter radical individualism. To be sure, sound doctrine is critical. As a pastor I believe this wholeheartedly — it's the reason I spent significant time in this book on the doctrines of original sin and union with Christ. However, if the church is to legitimatize solidarity, we must live in community with one another. We must *do* church in ways that are consistent with what we profess. We must know that we belong as bond servants to the Lord Jesus Christ. We must also truly conceive of ourselves as family, as brothers and sisters of one another, as fellow workers, as those who share the intimacy of a band of brothers fighting in an all-important battle.

The effectiveness of the early church in combining sound doctrine with plausibility structures is seen in the book of Acts. Consider Acts 2:42–47, a passage widely recognized as being paradigmatic for the New Testament church.[43] These verses outline those activities on which local churches should focus as they seek to be obedient to the Great Commission (see Matthew 28:18–20; Acts 1:6–8).

> And they devoted themselves to the apostles' teaching and fellowship, to the breaking of bread and the prayers. And awe came upon every soul, and many wonders and signs were being done through the apostles. And all who believed were together and had all things in common. And they were selling their possessions and belongings and distributing the proceeds to all, as any had need. And day by day, attending the temple together and breaking bread in their homes, they received their food with glad and generous hearts, praising God and having favor with all the people. And the Lord added to their number day by day those who were being saved.
>
> Acts 2:42–47

The central activities of the early church included the following:

- studying the **apostles' teaching**, that is, sound instruction from the Word of God
- **fellowship**, that is, *koinonia* — which carries the idea of sharing life together
- **breaking of bread**, which pertains to the Lord's Supper but also includes worship
- **prayer**

The church devoted itself to these activities. The verb translated "devoted" means "to attach one's self to."[44] It is in the present tense, and it carries the idea of ongoing action.[45] We could say, "The early church continued doing these things." They combined sound doctrine with their life together. Hence, the early church developed an alternative plausibility structure, a way of life that countered the culture in which they lived. The confession of the early church — salvation through Christ alone — was supported and buttressed by how they lived life together.

Similarly, Acts 4:32 – 37 emphasizes how the early church behaved in the context of community. In both passages there is an emphasis on what Robert Tannehill calls "communal living."[46] Of course, American capitalists get extremely nervous any time words like *communal* are thrown around, lest there be some sort of socialist agenda for the discussion. The point is not to prescribe a particular economic model.[47] Rather, we cannot overlook the fact that the early church was *sharing* life together. Christian community provides the vocabulary and categories for radical individualism to be countered.[48] No matter how much we may despise radical individualism, we will never be able to counter it apart from true community in the context of the local church. It is through the church that Jesus Christ is made visible in the world.

Like the apostle Paul, my prayer for you is that you will be active not only in nurturing the doctrinal knowledge of other believers but also in sharing life with them. Only by focusing on being together as a community of the redeemed to hear the Word proclaimed and to celebrate the sacraments together can churches counter the radical individualism of our day. Does the use of your time, treasure, and talents reflect that you know and understand that you are roped together with your local church?

A Final Summary

In *The Problem of Pain*, C. S. Lewis set out to write a Christian reflection on suffering. Soon enough, he arrived at the doctrine of original sin. Lewis summarized the truth that because of Adam's rebellion against God, "man is now a horror to God and to himself and a creature ill-adapted to the universe not because God made him so but because he has made himself so ..."[49]

Inevitably, a consideration of the doctrine of original sin brought Lewis face-to-face with the truth that all humanity was represented by Adam. Lewis allowed that it is hard for us to comprehend that Adam represented all his descendants, but he also noted that our inability to understand something does not mean it is untrue.

After all, Lewis pointed out, scientists readily admit they cannot understand everything physically: "We have recently been told by the scientists that we have no right to expect that the real universe should be picturable, and that if we make mental pictures to illustrate quantum physics, we are moving further away from reality, not nearer to it."[50] Lewis argued that if we cannot picture quantum physics exhaustively, we have even less reason to believe we should exhaustively understand the ways of God:

> We have clearly even less right to demand that the highest spiritual realities should be picturable, or even explicable in terms of our abstract thought ... That we can die "in" Adam and live "in" Christ seems to me to imply that man, as he really is, differs a good deal from man as our categories of thought and our three-dimensional imaginations represent him.[51]

Lewis then moved to the heart of the matter:

> The separateness — modified only by causal relations — which we discern between individuals, is balanced, in absolute reality, by some kind of "inter-inanimation" of which we have no conception at all. It may be that the acts and sufferings of great archetypal individuals such as Adam and Christ are ours, not by legal fiction, metaphor, or causality, but in some much deeper fashion. There is no question, of course, of individuals melting down into a kind of spiritual continuum such as Pantheistic systems believe in; that is excluded by the whole tenor of our faith. *But there may be a tension between individuality and some other principle.*[52]

Notice the emphasis here: *there may be a tension between individuality and some other principle.* I have named this principle "the principle of the rope." In a sense, this entire book has been an extended reflection on Lewis's observation that there must be some other principle. Summarized by chapter, the argument has developed as follows:

1. Like it or not, the principle of the rope or corporate solidarity is an undeniable aspect of life taught in Scripture. No man is an island. We are bound together.
2. The doctrine of original sin is the ultimate *negative* example of the principle of the rope. As *The New England Primer* summarizes, "In Adam's Fall/we sinned all."
3. Union with Christ is the ultimate *positive* example of the principle of the rope. Those who believe in Christ are united to him. And Christ's rope to save is stronger than Adam's rope is to condemn.
4. Scripture illustrates union with Christ by way of several key metaphors. We are united to Christ as stones to a temple, limbs to a body, branches to a vine, a wife to a husband, and adopted children to a father. Our relationship to Christ is even analogous to the relationships between the Father, Son, and Holy Spirit.
5. The principle of the rope does not teach fatalism, nor does it remove individual responsibility: "the soul who sins shall die" (Ezekiel 18:4). No one is necessarily doomed because of his or her parents.
6. Part 2 begins at chapter 6, where we considered the application of the principle of the rope. It follows from the truth that we are bound together in Christ that we experience true joy only as we invest ourselves in Christ-centered community.
7. Paul taught in Ephesians 5 that Christ's relationship with the church of corporate solidarity and a husband

and wife's bond in marriage explain one another. The principle of the rope allows us to better appreciate the loveliness of marriage and to understand the deep pain of divorce and death.

8. In terms of our families, we can be sure that the gospel rope is more powerful than the rope of sin. Live wholeheartedly for Christ; love him with all your heart, soul, strength, and mind—and know that God will do immeasurably more than all you can ask or imagine. But fear the consequences of turning your back on Almighty God, not only for yourself, but also for your family.

9. Christians can face death without fear because we have legitimate solidarity with a champion who has won the victory. For the Christian, there is nothing remote about Christ because we are united to him.

10. Only New Testament churches offer the theology combined with plausibility structures and the realities of community/fellowship necessary to legitimatize solidarity and counter the radical individualism unraveling the fabric of Western culture.

The heart of the matter is that because of the principle of the rope, it is possible to be united with Christ. And Christ's rope to save is stronger than Adam's rope is to condemn. Amazingly, gloriously, those who put their trust in Christ will be united together with him for all of eternity. Hence, this book, which began so deep in the woods, concludes with the certainty that those who are bound together with Christ will most certainly live with him, happily ever after, in a never-ending story "in which every chapter is better than the one before."[53]

Afterword

> One last thing must be said, a kind of warning. If those who hold influence over others fail to lead toward the spiritual uplands, then surely the path to the lowlands will be well worn. People travel together; no one lives detached and alone.
>
> J. Oswald Sanders, *Spiritual Leadership*

Don't get me wrong, we do need *individual* heroes.

Some may object that the emphasis on corporate solidarity in this book will undermine individual initiative and heroism. After all, Americans have a long history of believing in a mythic hero who is disconnected from the communities he rescues. The Lone Ranger, of course, is the quintessential example. No one knows his name. He wears a mask so the people do not know who he is or what he looks like. Astride Silver, he rides into town, solves the problem, and rides off ("Hi-yo, Silver! Away!") into the sunset before people even have the opportunity to thank him.

In one way or another, movies like *Shane* and *Pale Rider* reflect this "have gun, will travel" theme. More recently, Lee Child has written a popular fictional series about a mythic hero named Jack Reacher. Like the masked man, Reacher has no home. He does not carry a suitcase or do laundry. When he is done with a shirt, he buys a new one and throws the old one away. He wanders from one town to another, never establishing connections with people or developing long-term relationships. His family members are all dead. While Reacher does not treat the "school teacher" as honorably as the Lone Ranger did, he still avoids establishing any form of community with others.

Our culture idolizes the free-floating, unhindered, and isolated hero cut off from any formal responsibilities. But the Lone Ranger is a lie. Isolated heroes like Jack Reacher do not exist. Intentional isolation, far from inclining us to care for others and serve them, simply drives us deeper into our sinful, selfish patterns. It is nothing more than a comic-book myth that an emotionally isolated Batman would hop into the Batmobile and search out opportunities to help those in need. Because of our solidarity with Adam in sin, the Lone Ranger tendency is not to serve but to run. Lone Rangers will not lay down their lives for people with whom they have no connection. Lone Rangers don't fire their silver bullets for anyone but themselves.

The Bible teaches us that people are inspired to lay down their lives for others because they are connected to them in some way. The author of Hebrews writes, "By faith Moses, when he was grown up, refused to be called the son of Pharaoh's daughter, choosing rather to be mistreated *with the people of God* than to enjoy the fleeting pleasures of sin" (Hebrews 11:24–25, emphasis added). Ruth took the heroic action of leaving her people behind, not to become an isolated loner, but to become a part of Naomi's people, the Israelites. Her words, so beautifully rendered in the King James Version, read, "For whither thou goest, I will go; and where thou lodgest, I will lodge: thy people shall be my people, and thy God my God" (Ruth 1:16).

David challenged Goliath because Goliath picked a fight with the armies of the living God, and David felt bound to his people, jealous for his God. When Nehemiah sought to motivate to heroic action those who were rebuilding the wall, he reminded the people that they were *not* isolated individuals: "Do not be afraid of them. Remember the LORD, who is great and awesome, and fight for your brothers, your sons, your daughters, your wives, and your homes" (Nehemiah 4:14). And Esther's brave decision to risk her life by approaching the king was predicated on her love for her people, the Jews. She was willing to risk death for her people.

The heroic actions of individuals for the whole is something of a paradox. Biblical individualism happens when people see they are not isolated individuals. The true importance of an individual's actions lies in recognizing that they act for the sake of others, not for themselves. Of course, the greatest contrast to the mythic, individual hero is the Lord Jesus Christ. Although he is God, he made himself one of us. He took on the form of a servant and was born in the likeness of human beings (see Philippians 2:8). He established solidarity with us through his incarnation. Then, as the corporate head of the people of God, Christ succeeded where Adam failed, and those who place their faith and hope in him are united to him as their King. The lifeline he offers to those drowning in sin is stronger than Adam's rope.

I conclude with Psalm 20 — a *royal* psalm, a song in which the congregation prays a blessing for the king. It makes no sense when read as an individual; it assumes that those singing have embraced solidarity with their king.[1] The psalm enthusiastically proclaims, "O LORD, save the king!" Why? Because the people recognized that their fortunes and their future were tied to the king. Should the king succeed in battle, they would be victorious. Should the king receive the blessing of God, they, too, would receive God's blessing. As their leader, the king embodied the hopes of the people.

As subjects of King Jesus, we proclaim this psalm with a greater hope than the people of Israel who lived under the kings of old. We are confident our king has a throne that will last forever, that he has the favor of his Father, and has, even now, poured out the promised gift of the Spirit to sustain and strengthen his people, the church. Seated at the right hand of the throne of God, our King has freed us from the fear of death, and he is not ashamed to call us his brothers and sisters.

And he is coming again — soon.

> May the LORD answer you in the day of trouble!
>> May the name of the God of Jacob protect you!
> May he send you help from the sanctuary
>> and give you support from Zion!
> May he remember all your offerings
>> and regard with favor your burnt sacrifices!
> May he grant you your heart's desire
>> and fulfill all your plans!
> May we shout for joy over your salvation,
>> and in the name of our God set up our banners!
> May the LORD fulfill all your petitions!
> Now I know that the LORD saves his anointed;
>> he will answer him from his holy heaven
>> with the saving might of his right hand.
> Some trust in chariots and some in horses,
>> but we trust in the name of the LORD our God.
> They collapse and fall,
>> but we rise and stand upright.
> O LORD, save the king!
>> May he answer us when we call.

The Gospel and Assurance of Salvation

If you asked me, "What is your biggest fear as a pastor?" the answer would be easy. I fear for people in our flock who think they are Christians when they are not. Stating it baldly, some believe they are headed for heaven, but the reality is they are destined for hell. They think they are roped with Christ when they are not.

False assurance is a fact. Jesus warned that on the day of judgment he will say to many who think they are Christians, "I never knew you; depart from me" (Matthew 7:21 – 23). When they hear those terrible words, it will be the most terrible moment ever faced in human history.

The good news is we can have assurance of our salvation. Even as the New Testament exhorts us to examine ourselves to see whether we are in the faith (see 2 Corinthians 13:5), it also teaches there is a proper basis for assurance of salvation. You *can* be sure you will not be one of the people who hears, "I never knew you; depart from me." Indeed, God *wants* his people to have assurance of eternal life. The entire book of 1 John in the New Testament outlines the proper basis for assurance of salvation:

"I write these things to you who believe in the name of the Son of God that you may *know* that you have eternal life" (1 John 5:13, emphasis added).

How can you be sure you are truly a Christian? Begin by clearly understanding the gospel.

The Gospel

In 1 Corinthians 15:1 – 8 Paul summarizes the gospel:

> Now I would remind you, brothers, of the gospel I preached to you, which you received, in which you stand, and by which you are being saved, if you hold fast to the word I preached to you — unless you believed in vain.
>
> For I delivered to you as of first importance what I also received: that Christ died for our sins in accordance with the Scriptures, that he was buried, that he was raised on the third day in accordance with the Scriptures, and that he appeared to Cephas, then to the twelve. Then he appeared to more than five hundred brothers at one time, most of whom are still alive, though some have fallen asleep. Then he appeared to James, then to all the apostles. Last of all, as to one untimely born, he appeared also to me.
>
> 1 Corinthians 15:1 – 8

In this passage, consider four aspects of the gospel or good news:

1. The gospel was planned. Paul said that Christ died for our sins "in accordance with the Scriptures." Before the foundation of the world, God knew how he would rescue his people and his creation from sin and destruction. So even in Genesis 3:14 – 15, we have the protevangelium, or the first statement of the gospel, when God promises that the seed of the woman will crush the head of the serpent. God later promises Abraham that all nations will be blessed through him (Genesis 12:1 – 3). Isaiah proclaims the good news of Christ seven hundred years prior to the time of Christ (Isaiah 52:13 – 53:12). After the resurrection, Jesus explained on the road to Emmaus how all the Scriptures pointed to his death, burial, and resurrection (Luke 24:27).

2. The gospel is centered on the death, burial, and resurrection of Jesus. Christ died for our sins in accordance with the Scriptures. He was buried. He rose again. And many people saw him, touched him, talked with him, and ate with him after his resurrection. These things really happened. These historical events are the reality on which the good news is based.

3. The gospel proclaims that Christ paid the penalty for the sins of his people. All have sinned and fall short of the glory of God. The only way that sinful people can justly spend eternity with God is if the penalty for their sin is paid. This is why Paul stressed, "Christ died for our sins in accordance with the Scriptures." John adds, "In this is love, not that we have loved God but that he loved us and sent his Son to be the propitiation for our sins (1 John 4:10).

4. The gospel requires that salvation must be received by saving faith. Notice Paul's "if": "which you received, in which you stand, and by which you are being saved, *if* you hold fast to the word I preached to you — unless you believed in vain" (1 Corinthians 15:1 – 2, emphasis added). The gospel does not mean *everyone* is saved. Only those who turn in repentance from their sin and trust in Christ for the gift of eternal life are saved.

Paul says you are saved by faith if you hold fast to the Word. Saving faith is accompanied by a changed life. The grace of God that saves also sanctifies (Titus 2:11 – 14). "If anyone is in Christ, he is a new creation" (2 Corinthians 5:17). As surely as God made little green apples from little green apple trees, his grace will result in Christlike fruit in the life of a believer (Matthew 7:16). As the Reformers taught, "We are justified by faith alone, but not by a faith that is alone."

The Proper Basis for Assurance of Salvation

How can you be sure you are truly a Christian? You can evaluate whether you are forgiven by God by asking yourself three questions that are of vital importance. Don't ask yourself just one of them, but all three:

1. Do you presently have faith in the Lord Jesus for salvation?

Do you *presently* trust in Christ, and him alone, for eternal life? You may be able to identify a time when you turned in faith to Christ. Looking back at that point ought to be a great blessing. The more important question is, "Do you trust Jesus *today* for eternal life?" True saving faith is not something that comes and goes. If we truly have faith, then we will *continue* to have faith (1 Corinthians 15:1–2; Colossians 1:23; Hebrews 3:14). Wayne Grudem sums this up:

> Therefore a person should ask him or herself, "Do I today have trust in Christ to forgive my sins and take me without blame into heaven forever? Do I have confidence in my heart that he has saved me? If I were to die tonight and stand before God's judgment seat, and if he were to ask me why he should let me into heaven, would I begin to think of my good deeds and depend on them, or would I without hesitation say that I am depending on the merits of Christ and am confident that he is a sufficient Savior?"[1]

This emphasis on *present* faith in Christ stands in contrast to the practice of some church "testimonies" in which people repeatedly recite details of a conversion experience that may have happened twenty or thirty years ago. If a testimony of saving faith is genuine, it should be a testimony of faith that is active this very day.

2. Does the Holy Spirit testify with your spirit that you are a Christian?

The apostle Paul writes, "The Spirit himself bears witness with our spirit that we are children of God" (Romans 8:16). If you are truly a Christian, the Holy Spirit will give you an inner confidence that you know Christ.

This question is the most difficult to answer. You could drive yourself crazy as you ask yourself, "Is that the Spirit testifying with my spirit? Do I truly have a sense of the presence of Christ in my life?"

If you are a Christian, the Bible says God has poured out his love into your heart (see Romans 5:5). Douglas Moo adds:

> The confidence we have for the day of judgment is not based only on our intellectual recognition of the fact of God's love, or even only on the demonstration of God's love on the cross ... but on the inner, subjective certainty that God does love us ... and it is this internal, subjective — yes, even emotional — sensation within the believer that God does indeed love us — love expressed and made vital in real, concrete actions on our behalf — that gives to us the assurance that "hope will not disappoint us."[2]

If you are truly forgiven, you are a new creation in Christ (2 Corinthians 5:16 – 17), and the Spirit will testify with your spirit.

3. Does your conduct give evidence that you are a Christian?

If you are truly a Christian, you should act like it. The apostle John wrote, "By this we know that we have come to know him, if we keep his commandments. Whoever says 'I know him' but does not keep his commandments is a liar, and the truth is not in him" (1 John 2:3 – 4).

Now let us be clear. Acting like a Christian *does not make you* a Christian. However, true Christians act like Christians. As I said in chapter 10, quacking doesn't make you a duck, but ducks do quack. Holding pears in your hands does not make you a pear tree, but pear trees do hold pears. Acting like a Christian does not make you one, but Christians do act like Christians. Solomon wrote, "Even a child makes himself known by his acts, by whether his conduct is pure and upright" (Proverbs 20:11).

If your conduct consistently is not honoring to Christ, you should question your salvation. If you profess Christ and yet are content to live your life with no consistent local church involvement, you should question your salvation. If you are unwilling to identify with Christ in believer's baptism, you should question your salvation. If you persist in habitual sin, you should question your salvation. If these things characterize you, you should seriously question whether you are truly forgiven by God.

In order to evaluate whether you are truly a Christian, ask yourself these three questions:

1. Do I have present faith in the Lord Jesus Christ for salvation?
2. Does the Holy Spirit testify with my spirit that I am a Christian?
3. Is there evidence in my life that I am different because of my faith?

You may be saying, "Well, I've tried to evaluate myself in each of these three areas, and yet I'm still unsure. What do I do next?" I would encourage you to talk with someone who is a mature, Bible-believing Christian. Beyond that, the best thing you can do if you are unsure about your salvation is to get busy living the Christian life. Get involved in a Christ-centered, Bible-believing church. Start reading the Bible. Pray consistently. Ask God to give you confidence in your salvation. Take Jesus' yoke upon you, and learn from him (see Matthew 11:29).*

---

* Portions of this appendix are adapted from my book *Unpacking Forgiveness*.

For Further Reading

While not exhaustive, this list should be helpful in pointing readers to a number of excellent resources. By listing a source, I do not mean to imply I am in complete agreement. Rather, "test everything; hold fast what is good" (1 Thessalonians 5:21).

Original Sin

Jacobs, Alan. *Original Sin: A Cultural History*. New York: Harper Collins, 2008.

Johnson, Marcus. "A Way Forward on the Question of the Transmission of Original Sin." In *Evangelical Calvinism: Essays Resourcing the Continuing Reformation of the Church*. Edited by Myk Habets and Bobby Grow. Princeton Theological Monograph Series. Eugene, Oregon: Pickwick, 2012.

Murray, John. *Redemption Accomplished and Applied*. Grand Rapids: Eerdmans, 1955.

————*The Imputation of Adam's Sin*. Grand Rapids: Eerdmans, 1959.

Union with Christ

Billings, Todd J. *Union with Christ: Reframing Theology and Ministry for the Church*. Grand Rapids: Baker, 2011.

Letham, Robert. *Union with Christ: In Scripture, History, and Theology*. Phillipsburg, N.J.: P&R, 2011.

Biblical and Systematic Theology

Beale, G. K. *A New Testament Biblical Theology: The Unfolding of the Old Testament in the New*. Grand Rapids: Baker, 2011.

Grudem, Wayne A. *Systematic Theology: An Introduction to Biblical Doctrine*. Grand Rapids: Zondervan, 1994.

Horton, Michael. *The Christian Faith: A Systematic Theology for Pilgrims on the Way*. Grand Rapids: Zondervan, 2011.

Lloyd-Jones, D. Martyn. *Exposition of Romans 5: Assurance*. Volume 4 of *Romans*. Edinburgh: Banner of Truth, 2003.

Regarding the Destruction of the Canaanites

Gundry, Stanley N., ed. *Show Them No Mercy: 4 Views on God and Canaanite Genocide*. Grand Rapids: Zondervan, 2003.

Wright, Christopher J. H. *The God I Don't Understand: Reflections on Tough Questions of Faith*. Grand Rapids: Zondervan, 2008.

The Church

Clowney, Edmund P., and Gerald Lewis Bray. *The Church*. Contours of Christian Theology. Downers Grove, Ill.: InterVarsity, 1995.

Dever, Mark. *The Church: The Gospel Made Visible*. Nashville: Broadman & Holman, 2012.

Wells, David F. *Losing Our Virtue: Why the Church Must Recover Its Moral Vision*. Grand Rapids: Eerdmans, 1998.

On Marriage and the Family

Brauns, Chris. *Unpacking Forgiveness: Biblical Answers for Complex Questions and Deep Wounds*. Wheaton, Ill.: Crossway, 2008.

Keller, Timothy, and Kathy Keller. *The Meaning of Marriage: Facing the Complexities of Commitment with the Wisdom of God*. New York: Dutton, 2011.

Kostenberger, Andreas J., and David W. Jones. *God, Marriage, and Family: Rebuilding the Biblical Foundation*. 2nd ed. Wheaton, Ill.: Crossway, 2010.

Miller, C. John, and Barbara Miller Juliani. *Come Back, Barbara*. 2nd ed. Phillipsburg, N.J.: P&R, 1998.

Wilson, Douglas. *Federal Husband*. Moscow, Idaho: Canon, 1999.

Sociology and Political History

Bellah, Robert N., Richard Madsen, William M. Sullivan, Ann Swidler, and Steven M. Tipton. *Habits of the Heart: Individualism and Commitment in American Life*. Berkeley: University of California Press, 2008.

Berger, Peter L. *The Sacred Canopy: Elements of a Sociological Theory of Religion*. New York: Anchor, 1990.

Fea, John. *Was America Founded as a Christian Nation? A Historical Introduction*. Louisville: Westminster John Knox, 2011.

Hunter, James Davison. *To Change the World: The Irony, Tragedy, and Possibility of Christianity in the Late Modern World*. Oxford: Oxford University Press, 2010.

Kidd, Thomas S. *God of Liberty: A Religious History of the American Revolution*. New York: Basic Books, 2010.

Smith, Christian, Kari Christoffersen, Hilary Davidson, and Patricia Snell Herzog. *Lost in Transition: The Dark Side of Emerging Adulthood*. Oxford: Oxford University Press, 2011.

Smith, Christian, and Melinda Lundquist Denton. *Soul Searching: The Religious and Spiritual Lives of American Teenagers*. Oxford: Oxford University Press, 2005.

Smith, Christian, and Patricia Snell. *Souls in Transition: The Religious and Spiritual Lives of Emerging Adults*. Oxford: Oxford University Press, 2009.

Tocqueville, Alexis de. *Democracy in America*. Translated by Arthur Goldhammer. New York: Library of America, 2004.

Acknowledgments

It would be terribly ironic to write a book on solidarity without acknowledging that I am bound together with many who bring joy to my life. Of course, this begins with our King, the Lord Jesus Christ, but by definition it also includes his body, the church.

In Stillman Valley, Illinois, I am thankful to be one of the "bricks" mortared into the community of the Red Brick Church. As always, our administrative assistant, Jana Krause, reminds me to remember, even as she gets it done. Clayton Midtsem need not read this book since he has heard me discuss every page of it, even as we reflected on the tragic history of the Chicago Cubs. Shawn Ross led our deacons during most of this project and was usually willing to fall on whatever grenades were tossed into my study. Scott Groom and Jon Underhill came to the party late, but their sharp thinking has blessed me. Jamie and I are thankful for our pastoral renewal team of Pete Mazanec, Ken Mrozek, and Kay Swanson. As for our wider community in the Valley, at Three Sisters the coffee was good and Cheryl was willing to talk me through a paragraph when I got stuck. Meff and his forces at the Royal Blue are always friendly. If you stop by the Royal Blue, I recommend a cup of hot coffee along with the bacon and eggs.

This is my third book, and prior to writing, I had no idea how many people work behind the scenes for a title to be published. I am thankful for my agent, Tim Beals, and Credo

Communications. At Zondervan, Ryan Pazdur and Madison Trammel believed in this project from the beginning, and Andrew Rogers helped put the package together. Ryan has worked so hard on this project. Elsewhere, my good friend Dave De Wit encouraged me immensely as I developed this project across several years (Romans 15:13). Rick Wells continues to supply the grit needed to polish the stones until they are somewhat smooth (Proverbs 27:17).

During the final year of my Masters of Divinity program at Grand Rapids Theological Seminary, Dr. Jim Grier required us to write a paper about themes of coherence in biblical theology. One of the themes I chose to write about was solidarity, and the seed of that assignment continued to grow over the next twenty years and ultimately has become this book. For my Doctor of Ministry degree, I had the opportunity to study with Haddon Robinson, which has been an immense privilege. A group of us who graduated from the program continue to meet annually with Haddon at Lake Geneva, and my time together with friends like Tom Anderst, Darryl Dash, and Lamonte King is a wonderful blessing.

I have interacted with so many others about the theological content of this book. Mike Wittmer, Shannon ("Queen Archer") Popkin, Chip Bernhard, Steve Brandon, Bob Bixby, Jeremy Scott, Caleb Kolstad, Lance Mennen, Bruce McKanna, Jeremy Carr, and Larry Pauley have all encouraged me.

This book is dedicated to my children, and to all our family. Both my mother, Sharon McElhinney Galloway, and mother-in-law, Helen Baier Limbaugh, provided quiet contexts for writing. Unbelievably, my sister Mary Dawn still laughs at my jokes, and my sister Shelley sometimes returns my phone calls and commiserates. It is a shame I could not incorporate some sort of deer-hunting illustration for my brother Danny, the greatest hunter on earth, or make a reference to the Ottumwa National baseball victory for Rusty. I fully expect my loyal sister Erin to be in charge of marketing this book. Hardly a day goes by that I am not inspired by my father's work ethic. My cousin Tim encourages me, even though he is famous. Melanie understands. Jim can rest easy, knowing that my lips are sealed about the pig and that he and I will always have Rome. My aunts, Zelda and Virginia, are willing to bounce ideas around with me and assure me that my grandparents, Clyde and Mary Latha Campbell McElhinney, would be proud, which means the world. Our Covenanter ancestors came to Iowa in 1840. Their first priority was to establish a church. Given their commitment to federal theology, I'm sure they would be pleased with the "true blue" subject of this book, and I look forward very soon (Revelation 22:20) to enjoying corporate solidarity with them on the other side.

Our four children are an ongoing joy and delight. According to the sociologists, there is a declining work ethic in young people today. But as I write these words at 10:40 a.m., our oldest daughter, Allison, is working at her part-time job at the Julia Hull District Library, Christopher and Benjamin have the lawn mowers going (I promise to get a new battery, or at least charge the one we have), and our little girl, Mary Beth, has the best pumpkin patch anywhere in the Midwest, and she prays so faithfully. I cannot express what a joy it is to be in solidarity with such wonderful children who are so much a part of my writing. As always, I am so thankful for Jamie, my pretty, smiling wife. For her, I remain warm ...

Notes

Introduction: A Fairy-Tale Beginning

1. Frederick Buechner, *Telling the Truth: The Gospel as Tragedy, Comedy & Fairy Tale* (San Francisco: HarperSanFrancisco, 1977), 82.

Chapter One: Strange and Troubling Truth

1. Herman Melville, *Moby-Dick: or, The Whale* (New York: Penguin, 2001), 349.
2. "Therefore, I saw that here was a sort of interregnum in Providence; for its evenhanded equity never could have sanctioned so gross an injustice" (ibid).
3. Scot McKnight, "God's Wrath: A Question," *Jesus Creed*, May 23, 2008, www.patheos.com/blogs/jesuscreed/2008/05/23/gods-wrath-a-question/ (accessed August 14, 2012).
4. See John M. Frame, *The Doctrine of the Word of God* (Phillipsburg, N.J.: P&R, 2010), 4.
5. Michael Horton, *The Christian Faith: A Systematic Theology for Pilgrims on the Way* (Grand Rapids: Zondervan, 2012), 424.

Chapter Two: Original Rope

1. Francis Brown, S. R. Driver, and Charles Briggs, *A Hebrew and English Lexicon of the Old Testament* (Oxford: Clarendon, 1979), 374.
2. Anthony A. Hoekema, *Created in God's Image* (Grand Rapids: Eerdmans, 1994), 13; see Brown, Driver, and Briggs, *Hebrew and English Lexicon*, 853.
3. Brown, Driver, and Briggs, *Hebrew and English Lexicon*, 198.
4. Quoted in Hoekema, *Created in God's Image*, 65.
5. G. K. Beale, *A New Testament Biblical Theology: The Unfolding of the Old Testament in the New* (Grand Rapids: Baker, 2011), 34.

6. Michael Horton, *The Christian Faith: A Systematic Theology for Pilgrims on the Way* (Grand Rapids: Zondervan, 2012), 411.

7. Alan Jacobs, *Original Sin: A Cultural History* (New York: HarperCollins, 2008), 10 – 11.

8. *The Westminster Confession of Faith and Catechisms as Adopted by the Orthodox Presbyterian Church with Proofs Texts* (Willow Grove, Pa.: Committee on Christian Education of the Orthodox Presbyterian Church, 2005), 26 – 27, emphasis added, www.opc.org/documents/CFLayout.pdf (accessed August 14, 2012).

9. John Calvin, *Commentary on the Book of Psalms* (Edinburgh: Calvin Translation Society, 1847), 291.

10. See D. Martyn Lloyd-Jones, *Exposition of Romans 5: Assurance*, vol. 4 of *Romans* (Edinburgh: Banner of Truth, 2003), 218.

11. Jonathan Edwards, *The Great Christian Doctrine of Original Sin Defended*, vol. 1 of *The Works of Jonathan Edwards* (Edinburgh: Banner of Truth, 1834), 200. For an accessible and concise summary of Edwards's work on original sin, see George M. Marsden, *Jonathan Edwards: A Life* (New Haven, Conn.: Yale University Press, 2003), 447 – 58. See Paul Helm's balanced and helpful critique in "The Great Christian Doctrine (Original Sin)," in *A God Entranced Vision of All Things: The Legacy of Jonathan Edwards*, ed. John Piper and Justin Taylor (Wheaton, Ill.: Crossway, 2004), 175 – 200.

12. Marcus Johnson, "A Way Forward on the Question of the Transmission of Original Sin," in *Evangelical Calvinism: Essays Resourcing the Continuing Reformation of the Church*, ed. Myk Habets and Bobby Grow, Princeton Theological Monograph Series (Eugene, Ore.: Pickwick, 2012).

13. See Bruce Waltke, *Old Testament Theology* (Grand Rapids: Zondervan, 2007), 278.

14. See, for example, Psalm 20, quoted at the end of this book.

15. Douglas J. Moo, *The Epistle to the Romans* (New International Commentary on the New Testament; Grand Rapids: Eerdmans, 1996), 328, n. 61.

16. Lloyd-Jones, *Exposition of Romans 5*, 217 – 18.

17. Dorothy Sayers, *Letters to a Diminished Church: Passionate Arguments for the Relevance of Christian Doctrine* (Nashville: Nelson, 2004), 49.

18. Ibid., 65.

19. Jacobs, *Original Sin*, iv; see Bernard Ramm, *Offense to Reason: A Theology of Sin* (Vancouver, B.C.: Regent College Publishing, 1985).

Chapter Three: The Rope That Is Stronger

1. Fyodor Dostoyevsky, *The Brothers Karamazov*, trans. Richard Pevear and Larissa Volokhonsky (New York: Farrar, Straus and Giroux, 1991), 244.

2. See Joseph Frank, *Dostoevsky: A Writer in His Time*, abridged ed. (Princeton, N.J.: Princeton University Press, 2009), 789.

3. Dostoyevsky, *Brothers Karamazov*, 242.

4. Ibid., 244.

5. Ibid., 245.

6. D. Martyn Lloyd-Jones, *Exposition of Romans 5: Assurance*, vol. 4 of *Romans* (Edinburgh: Banner of Truth, 2003), 176, 180.

7. Douglas J. Moo, *The Epistle to the Romans*, New International Commentary on the New Testament (Grand Rapids: Eerdmans, 1996), 318.

8. "And Can It Be That I Should Gain," lyrics by Charles Wesley (1738).

Chapter Four: Bound to a New King

1. John Calvin, *Institutes of the Christian Religion*, ed. John T. McNeill, Library of Christian Classics (Philadelphia: Westminster, 1960), 1:737.

2. John Murray, *Redemption Accomplished and Applied* (Grand Rapids: Eerdmans, 1955), 201, 205.

3. Robert Letham, *Union with Christ: In Scripture, History, and Theology* (Phillipsburg, N.J.: P&R, 2011), 1.

4. Murray, *Redemption Accomplished and Applied*, 166.

5. See Archibald Alexander Hodge, *Outlines of Theology* (New York: Hodder & Stoughton, 1878), 370.

6. Murray, *Redemption Accomplished and Applied*, 167.

7. Abraham Kuyper, *The Holy Spirit* (Chattanooga, Tenn.: AMG, 1995), 349.

8. See Hodge, *Outlines of Theology*, 370.

9. Charles Spurgeon, "In Christ No Condemnation," in *The Metropolitan Tabernacle Pulpit: Sermons, Parts 369–380* (London: Passmore and Alabaster, 1886), 475.

10. Murray, *Redemption Accomplished and Applied*, 168.

11. Henri Blocher writes, "An additional comment could be made on the structure which binds the spiritual oneness of humankind while maintaining individual distinction. It may belong to the reflection or traces of the Trinity one can find in creation (*vestigial trinitatis*). As one climbs the scale of created being, individual distinction and unity grow together — pointing, perhaps, to the mystery of the absolute distinction of the Three within the absolute unity of the one divine essence (*Original Sin: Illuminating the Riddle* [Downers Grove, Ill.: InterVarsity, 1997], 98–99).

12. Letham, *Union with Christ*, 37.

13. D. Martyn Lloyd-Jones, *Exposition of Romans 5: Assurance*, vol. 4 of *Romans* (Edinburgh: Banner of Truth, 2003), 219.

Chapter Five: Can We Blame the Rope?

1. See Walter C. Kaiser Jr., *The History of Israel: From the Bronze Age Through the Jewish War* (Nashville: Broadman & Holman, 1998), 393.

2. See Daniel I. Block, *The Book of Ezekiel, Chapters 1–24,* New International Commentary on the Old Testament (Grand Rapids: Eerdmans, 1997), 563.

3. See ibid., 557.

4. John M. Frame, *The Doctrine of the Christian Life* (Phillipsburg, N.J.: P&R, 2008), 260.

5. Ibid., 265.

Chapter Six: Bound Together for Joy

1. G. K. Chesterton, *Orthodoxy* (New York: Doubleday, 1959), 4.

2. Ibid., 1.

3. Blaise Pascal, *Pascal's Pensees,* trans. W. F. Trotter (New York: Dutton, 1958), 113, thought #425.

4. William Tyndale, from his prologue to the New Testament, 1525.

5. Jerry Bridges, *The Discipline of Grace: God's Role and Our Role in the Pursuit of Holiness* (Colorado Springs: NavPress, 1994), 45.

6. Ibid., 60.

7. C. S. Lewis, *The Weight of Glory and Other Addresses* (New York: Macmillan, 1949), 2.

8. D. Martyn Lloyd-Jones, *Fellowship with God* (Wheaton, Ill.: Crossway, 1993), 34.

9. See Bridges, *Discipline of Grace,* 72.

Chapter Seven: Bound Together in Marriage

1. See Bruce C. Waltke, *The Book of Proverbs, Chapters 15–31,* New International Commentary on the Old Testament (Grand Rapids: Eerdmans, 2005), 490.

2. See Timothy Keller and Kathy Keller, *The Meaning of Marriage: Facing the Complexities of Commitment with the Wisdom of God* (New York: Dutton, 2011), 47.

3. See my book *Unpacking Forgiveness: Biblical Answers for Complex Questions and Deep Wounds* (Wheaton, Ill.: Crossway, 2008), where I respond to the question "Must a person always stay married to a spouse who says he or she is repentant?"(p. 202).

4. See Stephen B. Clark, *Man and Woman in Christ: An Examination of the Roles of Men and Women in Light of Scripture and the Social Sciences* (Ann Arbor, Mich.: Servant, 1980), 82.

5. Keller and Keller, *Meaning of Marriage,* 241.

6. See John M. Frame, *The Doctrine of the Christian Life* (Phillipsburg, N.J.: P&R, 2008), 581.

7. "The Baptist Faith and Message," www.sbc.net/bfm/bfm2000.asp (accessed August 20, 2012).

8. D. Marty Lasley, "Keeping Women in Servitude Down on the Plantation: Why Southern Baptists Resurrected the Hermeneutics of Slavery."

9. John Calvin wrote, "We have seen so far how each of us is subject to his neighbours, and that we cannot otherwise live one with another, than by engaging in some duty in token of subjection. And since that does not please us, because each of us covets to be above his fellows, and since we set so much store by loftiness that it is hard for us to stoop, we have seen also that if we fear God we must not think it strange that we submit ourselves to our neighbors, for God created us with that condition in view" (*Sermons on the Epistle to the Ephesians* [Edinburgh: Banner of Truth, 1973], 564).

Chapter Eight: A Red Rope for Hurting Families

1. C. John Miller and Barbara Miller Juliani, *Come Back, Barbara*, 2nd ed. (Phillipsburg, N.J.: P&R, 1997), 37 – 38.

2. Christopher J. H. Wright, *The God I Don't Understand: Reflections on Tough Questions of Faith* (Grand Rapids: Zondervan, 2008), 93.

3. Tremper Longman III, "The Case for Spiritual Continuity," in *Show Them No Mercy: 4 Views on God and Canaanite Genocide*, ed. Stanley N. Gundry (Grand Rapids: Zondervan, 2003), 173 – 74.

4. Russell D. Moore, *Adopted for Life: The Priority of Adoption for Christian Families and Churches* (Wheaton, Ill.: Crossway, 2009), 37.

Chapter Nine: A Rescue Rope for Those Facing the Fear of Death

1. E. M. Blaiklock, "Nero," in *The Zondervan Encyclopedia of the Bible*, ed. Merrill C. Tenney, revision ed. Moisés Silva (Grand Rapids: Zondervan, 1975, 2009), 4:453 – 55.

2. I am taking my lead from the esteemed New Testament scholar William Lane, who contended that it was to this group — a small group of believers facing painful persecutions in or around Rome in AD 64 — that the book of Hebrews was written (William L. Lane, *Call to Commitment: Responding to the Message of Hebrews* [Nashville: Nelson, 1985], 22). Others argue for a different location (see, for example, Philip Edgecumbe Hughes, *A Commentary on the Epistle to the Hebrews* [Grand Rapids: Eerdmans, 1977]).

3. See Lane, *Call to Commitment*, 24 – 25.

4. See Peter T. O'Brien, *The Letter to the Hebrews* (Grand Rapids: Eerdmans, 2010), 105 – 6. The word translated "founder" appears in the New Testament three other times — each time it is used to describe Christ.

5. See George H. Guthrie, *Hebrews*, NIV Application Commentary (Grand Rapids: Zondervan, 1998), 117, 119.

6. For an explanation of this psalm as being prophetic of Christ's passion, see Bruce K. Waltke, James M. Houston, and Erika Moore, *The Psalms as Christian Worship: A Historical Commentary* (Grand Rapids: Eerdmans, 2010), 376–415.

7. Psalm 22:18 is quoted in John 19:24. Psalm 22:7 is alluded to in Matthew 27:39 and Mark 15:29. Psalm 22:1 is quoted in Matthew 27:46 and Mark 15:34.

8. See O'Brien, *Letter to the Hebrews*, 111; F. F. Bruce, *The Epistle to the Hebrews*, rev. ed., New International Commentary on the New Testament (Grand Rapids: Eerdmans, 1990), 82.

9. John Murray, *Collected Writings of John Murray: Lectures in Systematic Theology* (Edinburgh: Banner of Truth, 1977), 2:132.

10. *The Westminster Confession of Faith and Catechisms as Adopted by the Orthodox Presbyterian Church with Proofs Texts* (Willow Grove, Pa.: Committee on Christian Education of the Orthodox Presbyterian Church, 2005), 36, www.opc.org/documents/CFLayout.pdf (accessed August 14, 2012).

11. Robert Letham, *Union with Christ: In Scripture, History, and Theology* (Phillipsburg, N.J.: P&R, 2011), 53.

12. See Lane, *Call to Commitment*, 46.

13. John Calvin, *Institutes of the Christian Religion*, ed. John T. McNeill, Library of Christian Classics (Philadelphia: Westminster, 1960), 1:92.

14. Gerry Breshears, "The Body of Christ: Prophet, Priest or King?" *Journal of the Evangelical Theological Society* 37.1 (1994): 17.

15. Frederick Dale Bruner, *The Christbook*, vol. 1 of *Matthew: A Commentary*, rev. ed. (Grand Rapids: Eerdmans, 2007), 120.

16. Helmuth James von Moltke, *Letters to Freya: 1939–1945*, ed. Beate Ruhm von Oppen (New York: Knopf, 1990), 406.

17. Ibid., 410–11.

Chapter Ten: Roped Together in Country and Culture

1. The author of Chronicles terms those from the tribe of Issachar as "men who had understanding of the times, to know what Israel ought to do" (1 Chronicles 12:32).

2. See Christian Smith et al., *Lost in Transition: The Dark Side of Emerging Adulthood* (Oxford: Oxford University Press, 2011), 239. "It is not the normal business of sociologists to prescribe normative responses to the social realities they study. It is better, we generally think, to simply describe and explain the social world to and for others, and then to let various kinds of readers figure out what, if anything, they want to do about it."

3. Alexis de Tocqueville, *Democracy in America*, trans. Arthur Goldhammer (New York: Library of America, 2004), 322.

4. Ibid., 323.
5. Ibid., 331.
6. Thomas Kidd writes, "Despite his sanguine view of American religion, Tocqueville was personally skeptical about Christianity. Early in his life he became a deist, and for most of his life he did not receive communion as a Catholic. Nevertheless, he always maintained a general belief in God, Providence, and an afterlife. In this combination of personal doubt but public support for religion, Tocqueville manifested a view of religion not unlike that of several prominent founding fathers, including Jefferson. Jefferson and Tocqueville personally abandoned traditional orthodoxy, while maintaining that it was essential for the masses to keep believing in Christianity — or at least in good and evil — and in eternal rewards in the afterlife" (*God of Liberty: A Religious History of the American Revolution* [New York: Basic Books, 2010], 248).
7. Tocqueville, *Democracy in America*, 336.
8. Ibid., 337.
9. See Kidd, *God of Liberty*; Mark A. Noll, *The Rise of Evangelicalism: The Age of Edwards, Whitefield and the Wesleys* (Downers Grove, Ill.: InterVarsity, 2010); John Fea, *Was America Founded as a Christian Nation? A Historical Introduction* (Louisville: Westminster John Knox, 2011); Michael S. Horton, *Made in America: The Shaping of Modern American Evangelicalism* (Eugene, Ore.: Wipf & Stock, 1998).
10. Tocqueville, *Democracy in America*, 14.
11. Samuel Gregg, "Socialism and Solidarity," *The City* (Spring 2011): 63, www.thepublicdiscourse.com/2010/12/2169 (accessed August 22, 2012).
12. Tocqueville, *Democracy in America*, 331.
13. Ibid., 337.
14. Ibid., 336.
15. Ibid., 708.
16. "Washington's Farewell Address 1796," Avalon Project, http://avalon.law .yale.edu/18th_century/washing.asp (accessed August 22, 2012).
17. Tocqueville, *Democracy in America*, 585.
18. Ibid., 709.
19. Ibid., 818.
20. Ibid.
21. Robert Bellah et al. call radical individualism "ontological individualism." They write, "The essence of the Lockean position is an almost ontological individualism. The individual is prior to society, which comes into existence only through the voluntary contract of individuals trying to maximize their own self-interest." They add that ontological individualism is "a belief that the individual has a primary reality whereas society is a second-order, derived or artificial construct, a view we can call *ontological individualism*. This view is shared by utilitarian and expressive

segmentpage>`

individualists. It is opposed to the view that society is as real as individuals, a view we call *social realism*, which is common to the biblical and republican traditions" (*Habits of the Heart: Individualism and Commitment in American Life* (Berkeley: University of California Press, 2008), ix, 334.

22. Tocqueville, *Democracy in America*, 818.

23. Ibid.

24. See D. A. Carson, "Contrarian Reflections on Individualism," *Themelios* 35.3 (2010): 378–83; Jonathan Leeman, "Individualism's Not the Problem—Community's Not the Solution," *Modern Reformation* 17.4 (2008): 27–31.

25. David F. Wells, *Losing Our Virtue: Why the Church Must Recover Its Moral Vision* (Grand Rapids: Eerdmans, 1998), 67.

26. Scot McKnight, "Self in a Castle," *Out of Ur*, August 28, 2009, www.outofur.com/archives/2009/08/scot_mcknight_s.html.

27. Christian Smith and Patricia Snell, *Souls in Transition: The Religious and Spiritual Lives of Emerging Adults* (Oxford: Oxford University Press, 2009), 49.

28. Christian Smith and Melinda Lundquist Denton, *Soul Searching: The Religious and Spiritual Lives of American Teenagers* (Oxford: Oxford University Press, 2005), 143.

29. Bellah et al., *Habits of the Heart*, 144.

30. Smith et al., *Lost in Transition*, 225.

31. Robert H. Bork, *Slouching Towards Gomorrah: Modern Liberalism and American Decline* (New York: HarperCollins, 2003), 6.

32. Carson, "Contrarian Reflections on Individualism," 378, 380; he goes on to warn that we need to be careful we don't displace the basic theological analysis by turning individualism into the primary bogeyman.

33. Robert Bork writes, "One would have expected rejection of radical individualism and radical egalitarianism by those whose interests would be damaged by them or whose idea of a good society was offended by them. Instead, resistance has been mild, disorganized, and ineffective" (*Slouching Towards Gomorrah*, 7).

34. Quoted in Albert Mohler, "Rethinking Secularization: A Conversation with Peter Berger," www.albertmohler.com/2010/10/11/rethinking-secularization-a-conversation-with-peter-berger-2/ (accessed August 22, 2012). Berger writes, "The world-building activity of man is always and inevitably a collective enterprise. While it may be possible, perhaps for heuristic purposes, to analyze man's relationship to his world in purely individual terms, the empirical reality of human world-building is always a social one. Men together shape tools, invent languages, adhere to values, devise institutions, and so on" (*The Sacred Canopy: Elements of a Sociological Theory of Religion* [New York: Anchor, 1990], 7).

35. James Davison Hunter, *To Change the World: The Irony, Tragedy, and Possibility of Christianity in the Late Modern World* (Oxford: Oxford University Press), 33.

36. Bellah et al., *Habits of the Heart*, 81.

37. Berger, *Sacred Canopy*, 51.

38. Berger writes, "Once produced, this world cannot simply be wished away. Although all culture originates and is rooted in the subjective consciousness of human beings, once formed it cannot be reabsorbed into consciousness at will. It stands outside the subjectivity of the individual, as indeed, a world. In other words, the humanly produced world attains the character of objective reality" (*Sacred Canopy*, 9).

39. Hunter, *To Change the World*, 202.

40. Ibid., 282–83.

41. See Walter Bauer et al., *A Greek-English Lexicon of the New Testament and Other Early Christian Literature*, 3rd ed. (Chicago: University of Chicago Press, 2000), 552–53.

42. Douglas Moo acknowledges that verse 6 is "universally recognized as the most difficult in Philemon." He brings together his exegetical conclusions by paraphrasing the verse: "Philemon, I am praying that the mutual participation that arises from your faith in Christ might become effective in leading you to understand and put into practice all the good that God wills for us and that is found in our community; and do all this for the sake of Christ" (*The Letters to the Colossians and to Philemon*, Pillar New Testament Commentary (Grand Rapids: Eerdmans, 2008], 384).

43. F. F. Bruce writes, "Luke presents in this paragraph an ideal picture of this new community ... This teaching was authoritative because it was the teaching of the Lord communicated through the apostles in the power of the Spirit. For believers of later generations the New Testament scriptures form the written deposit of the apostolic teaching" (*The Book of the Acts*, New International Commentary on the New Testament [Grand Rapids: Eerdmans, 1988], 73).

44. Bauer et al., *A Greek-English Lexicon*, 715.

45. Nigel Turner, *Grammar of New Testament Greek* (Edinburgh: T&T Clark, 1963), 60.

46. Robert C. Tannehill, *The Narrative Unity of Luke-Acts: A Literary Interpretation* (Philadelphia: Fortress, 1986), 43.

47. See Gregg, "Socialism and Solidarity."

48. See Hunter, *To Change the World*, 254.

49. C. S. Lewis, *The Problem of Pain* (New York: HarperCollins, 2001), 63.

50. Ibid., 82–83.

51. Ibid., 83.

52. Ibid., emphasis added.

53. C. S. Lewis, *The Last Battle* (The Chronicles of Narnia; New York: Macmillan, 1970), 184.

Afterword

1. Regarding Psalm 20, Willem VanGemeren writes, "Concern for God's blessing on the king in facing national distress dominates the psalm. It contains a beautiful expression of solidarity between the people and their king, as all are involved in imploring the Lord's favor. The people recognize the anointed leader as God's agent in bestowing his favor on the people" (*Psalms*, Expositors Bible Commentary [Grand Rapids: Zondervan, 2008], 223). Regarding Psalm 40, Peter Craigie writes, "The interrelationship is to be found in the king's representative role, for within the covenant context, he carried individually upon his shoulders the responsibility for his people. And his desire for the nation, as expressed in this liturgy of supplication, was deliverance or salvation (v. 14). Thus, implicit in the psalm is a principle of representation within the kingdom of God, though here the kingdom is in the form of a nation state, Israel (and/or, Judah). In one sense, every individual person shared in the covenant relationship with God. In another sense, given the context of kingdom, the relationship was channeled through the person of the king, for in a very real sense the future of the kingdom, as a national and political entity, depended on the king's role" (*Psalms 1–50*, Word Biblical Commentary [Waco, Tex.: Word, 1983], 317).

Appendix One: The Gospel and Assurance of Salvation

1. Wayne A. Grudem, *Systematic Theology: An Introduction to Biblical Doctrine* (Grand Rapids: Zondervan, 1994), 803.
2. Douglas Moo, *Romans 1–8*, Wycliffe Exegetical Commentary (Chicago: Moody, 1991), 312–13.